BEREAVEMENT

The Essential Guide

Need
— 2 —
Know

Laura
Cook

First published in Great Britain in 2009 by
Need2Know
Remus House
Coltsfoot Drive
Peterborough
PE2 9JX
Telephone 01733 898103
Fax 01733 313524
www.need2knowbooks.co.uk

Need2Know is an imprint of Forward Press Ltd.
www.forwardpress.co.uk
SB ISBN 978-1-86144-068-6
Cover photograph: Jupiter Images

Contents

In memory of Richard Cook

Introduction

At some point in our lives most of us will have to cope with the death of a loved one. The loss of a parent, child, friend, sibling, grandparent or partner can be devastating and may leave you feeling unable to cope. You might feel angry, numb, shocked, helpless, sad, guilty or even that you are going mad. Bereavement is one of the most painful experiences that any of us can face. Nevertheless, it is possible to lead a happy and fulfilling life, even in the absence of a loved one.

Having experienced bereavement myself, I hope that this book will help and support you in both the months and years following your loss. You may hear people say that grief is a very personal thing, but it is important to remember that you are not alone. Support is available from family and friends, counsellors, self-help groups (see help list) and your GP, as well as this book. You don't need to suffer in silence.

Losing someone is a terrible shock. Whether they have been ill for some months or have died suddenly, nothing can prepare you for their passing. It is natural to feel numb as you struggle to comprehend what has happened. You may also be surprised by your own reactions. If you consider yourself to be a patient, controlled person, it can be bewildering to feel furious one minute and tearful the next. If you are a naturally emotional person, you might be stunned and horrified to find that you cannot cry. All of these responses are normal and are not a sign that you are mad, uncaring or a bad person. This book offers practical strategies for coping with these difficult emotions.

After someone's death, there are many practical things to be done. Sadly, these tasks often have to be completed at a time when you feel least able to cope. Chapters 1 and 2 offer a simple and straightforward guide to making arrangements and managing legal issues surrounding the death of a loved one. Chapter 3 also offers advice on one of the hardest tasks – breaking the bad news to others, including children.

If you are reading this book as a friend or carer of someone who has been bereaved, chapter 8 will help you to offer both emotional and practical support to ease their burden. The fear of doing or saying the wrong thing can make it hard to talk to the bereaved individual, but avoiding them can be hurtful. As chapter 8 suggests, even small gestures can make a difference to the wellbeing of the bereaved person.

In some cases, the way in which someone has died can be particularly traumatic. Bereavement by suicide, childhood illness, accident or crime poses a set of unique challenges for those left behind. Chapter 9 offers advice to support you in dealing with these challenges.

It may not seem like it at the moment, but you can survive the death of someone close to you. Chapter 10 looks at ways of moving forward and making the most of your own life after bereavement. It is hoped that this book will help you to find enjoyment in life once again.

Disclaimer

This book offers general information on bereavement and is not intended to replace medical and professional advice, although it can be used alongside it. Anyone who suspects they are suffering from depression should seek medical advice from their GP in the first instance. Anyone experiencing suicidal thoughts should immediately seek advice from an A&E department, their GP or the Samaritans.

Chapter One

What To Do When Someone Dies

When someone dies, the last thing you may feel like is making arrangements, organising and completing paperwork. Unfortunately, however, there are a number of tasks that must be completed at this difficult time. If you are the next of kin, many of the official duties may fall to you. This does not mean, however, that you have to handle everything yourself – friends, neighbours and relatives can be asked to help, whether it's to locate the required documents or simply to provide moral support. Although it is a deeply sad time, some people find that arranging a funeral can bring about some relief, as it is the last thing they can do for a lost loved one. In this chapter, we'll look at some of the things that need to be handled immediately after and in the first week following the death of a loved one. These tasks include:

- Obtaining a medical certificate.
- Considering organ donation.
- Registering the death.
- Organising a funeral.

Depending on the circumstances surrounding the death, a coroner may need to be involved. This chapter will help you to understand:

- The role of the coroner.
- The reasons for conducting a post-mortem.
- What happens at an inquest.

'Although it is a deeply sad time, some people find that arranging a funeral can bring about some relief, as it is the last thing they can do for a lost loved one.'

The first few hours

When someone dies, their GP will issue a medical certificate specifying the cause of death. If the deceased is not registered with a local practice, or their GP is unavailable to attend, another GP will sign the form. It is vital to keep hold of the medical certificate as you will need it to register the death later on. In some cases, the GP may be unable to determine the cause of death. This might happen if the death:

- Occurred in suspicious circumstances.

- Was sudden, such as sudden infant death syndrome (SIDS).

- Is unexplained (when the GP in attendance cannot determine the cause).

'When someone dies, their GP will issue a medical certificate specifying the cause of death.'

- Was violent (involving a suspected crime).

- Was unnatural (through suicide or drug overdose).

- Was accidental (the result of an injury sustained at work or in the home).

- Happened in hospital (failure to recover from an anaesthetic or death during an operation).

- Was the result of an industrial hazard or accident.

- Took place in police custody or prison.

- If the deceased had not seen their GP or the attending GP in the 14 days before death.

If death has occurred in any of these circumstances, the GP (or attending police) will report the matter to a coroner – the GP will record that the case has been referred to a coroner on the medical certificate. You must wait for the verdict from the coroner before the death can be officially registered.

At this point, you may wish to inform other family members, friends and the deceased's place of work. If the death is not referred to the coroner, you can go on to register the death with the medical certificate of cause of death.

Considering organ donation

Depending on the circumstances, you may be asked to consider organ donation. This means that organs or tissue will be taken from the body of the deceased person so that they may be transplanted into someone else. There are many ill people on transplant waiting lists in the UK and donated organs are in short supply. For some bereaved people, it can be a comfort to know that their loss, although painful, has saved the life of someone else. The deceased person may have signed up to the organ donation register and may therefore carry a donor card in their purse or wallet. If not, the next of kin may make the decision on their behalf. The attending doctor will be able to advise you if donation is possible, and if so, what to do next.

Donation of the heart, kidneys, pancreas and lungs are (usually) only feasible where the donor's heartbeat and breathing have been maintained. For instance, organ donation is often possible where the donor is on a ventilator or in intensive care but brain stem death has been declared. Occasionally, it may be possible to use bone, skin, corneas and heart valves for transplantation up to a maximum of 72 hours after death. However, it is worth noting that where a death has been referred to a coroner, permission will be required before removal of organs can take place. Again, hospital staff and doctors will be able to advise you on the procedure.

'For some bereaved people, it can be a comfort to know that their loss, although painful, has saved the life of someone else.'

What happens to the body?

It may not be pleasant to think about, but the next thing to consider is what happens to the body. For some people, like Angela, it helps to know what is going to happen next:

'I found it difficult to understand what was going on because nobody told me what was going to happen. I couldn't understand why they wanted to take Roger's body away for tests when our family wanted to have the funeral.'

At this stage, don't be afraid to ask questions – it is important to understand what happens next.

The role of the coroner

The coroner is a lawyer (or sometimes a doctor) who has been appointed by the government to determine cause of death. They will also organise a post-mortem and further investigations (if they are judged to be necessary). If the death has been referred to the coroner because the deceased did not see their GP in the fortnight leading up to their death, but everything else is in order, a post-mortem is unlikely to be required. In this case, the coroner will release the body for burial and the death can be officially registered. If, however, death occurred unnaturally or in certain other circumstances (such as an accident or suicide) a post-mortem will need to be carried out.

What is a post-mortem?

A post-mortem is an examination of the deceased's body. Usually, tissue samples and other organs are removed by a pathologist for analysis. The results of these tests are used to determine cause (and in some cases the circumstances) of death. The thought of a post-mortem can be very upsetting for those left behind, but it is important to remember that there are strict guidelines determining the conditions in which these tests can be carried out. The dignity of the deceased is of paramount importance to the professionals involved.

This can be a difficult time as it can feel like you're in limbo, unable to start funeral arrangements or see the body. However, while you can't set a firm date for the service, you can use this time to discuss the type of funeral you would like and find a funeral director.

What are my rights?

- While you cannot refuse a post-mortem, you can express any concerns you may have to the coroner and inform them of any religious objections.
- You can elect someone to liaise with the coroner's office. This job usually falls to the next of kin, but you can ask for someone to do it on your behalf if this is either too difficult or not practicable.

- You are entitled to ask the coroner for a copy of the post-mortem findings (a small fee may be payable).

- You may begin to plan flowers, music and order of service for the funeral, even though the date cannot yet be set.

- You can request to have your choice of medical representative present at the post-mortem.

What happens next depends on the findings of the post-mortem. There are three possible outcomes – death is deemed as natural, unnatural or unexplained.

If the cause of death is deemed natural

The coroner will usually issue a notification (known as pink form B) to the registrar of deaths. Once the registrar has received this form you may register the death. Occasionally, and depending upon where you live, the coroner will send the notification (pink form B) to you to deliver to the registrar yourself. If the body of the deceased is to be cremated, the coroner will send the 'certificate for cremation' (to be passed to the registrar) which will allow this to take place.

If the cause of death is unnatural or unexplained

In cases of suicide, violence, death in police custody or where the post-mortem is inconclusive (fails to discover the cause of death), the coroner will order an inquest. However, providing that no further post-mortem investigations are required, the coroner can usually release the body for burial/cremation at this time. In order to help surviving relatives organise the will and funeral, an interim certificate of fact of death may be issued. If an inquest will be carried out, the coroner or coroner's office has a duty to inform:

- The husband, wife or civil partner of the deceased.

- The closest relative, if this differs from the above.

- The personal representative chosen by either of the above.

What is an inquest?

An inquest is a legal investigation that aims to clarify the circumstances surrounding a death. If the post-mortem was inconclusive, it may also try to establish the most likely cause of death. Inquests take place in a court of law, and the public are therefore able to attend. However, an inquest is not a trial, so no one will be blamed or held legally responsible for the death. If there is to be a criminal trial, it will be held after the inquest has taken place. Sometimes, the public nature of an inquest can seem to take matters out of your control. You can, however, choose to be as little or as fully involved in the proceedings as you wish.

What are my rights?

'An inquest is a legal investigation which aims to clarify the circumstances surrounding a death.'

- You or any of your family can attend.
- You are permitted to ask questions of the witnesses about the circumstances of the death.
- You can engage the services of a lawyer to ask questions on your behalf. You should, however, be aware that you will not be entitled to legal aid in this instance.
- You can also engage a lawyer where the proceedings might lead to a future claim for compensation, such as in the case of accidental death, criminal activity or as the result of negligence.

Registering a death

It is not necessary for the next of kin or nearest relative to register the death, although they are entitled to do so if they wish. Otherwise, there are a number of other people who may do so. These include:

- Another relative.
- Someone who was present at the death.
- A responsible member of staff from the deceased person's hospital or care home.

- Someone who lived with the deceased.

Whoever registers the death must be able to produce the medical certificate of cause of death. Where a post-mortem has taken place, the coroner will usually send the certificate to the registrar automatically, but it is important to check whether you still need to register the death in person. To register a death, you may be required to visit the local registrar of birth, deaths and marriages. Your local council will be able to advise you on location and opening hours. To register a death, you'll need to take the following documents with you:

- Medical certificate of cause of death, signed by the attending GP.
- If possible, the birth certificate of the deceased and any marriage/civil partnership certificates.
- Means of payment for copies of the death certificate.

These will provide the following information for the registrar:

- Full name of the deceased.
- Date and place of death.
- Date and place of birth.
- Maiden name(s).
- Marriage/civil partnership details.
- Occupation of spouse or civil partner.

What will the registrar ask me?

- The full names and address of the person registering the death.
- Any other names the deceased was known by.
- Questions about employment for government statistics.

You will be given:

- A white form (BD8 form) to send to the Department for Work and Pensions (DWP).
- A form to be given to the funeral director.
- Copies of the death certificate.

'The registrar's office is a useful information resource. You may ask for information leaflets on planning a funeral and covering expenses.'

The registrar's office is also a useful information resource. You may ask for information leaflets on planning a funeral and covering expenses.

What should I do next?

After you have registered the death, you will have been given a number of important documents by the registrar. The white form (known as BD8 in the UK) should be completed and sent off to the DWP. This will inform them to stop any benefits and calculate any taxes (or rebates) due to the deceased. If you haven't done so already, you should also attempt to find out whether the deceased person made a will.

If you are unsure whether the deceased made a will, you should contact the deceased's solicitor (if they have one). If the solicitor does not hold a copy, you will need to check through the personal documents of the deceased to rule out the existence of a will.

Organising a funeral

Once the death has been registered, you can set a date for the funeral and organise the service. It can be difficult to know where to start, especially when you are in shock or grieving, so it can be useful to break the arrangements down into small steps. Writing things down and making a list of jobs can help to order your thoughts, as well as help others to see areas in which you may need help.

Here are some of the first things you may need to consider:

- Did the deceased have a will, and if so, were any special arrangements made for the funeral?
- Where will the deceased remain until the funeral? Chapel of rest, funeral director or at home?
- Whether to opt for a burial or cremation.
- The type of funeral service you wish to hold, i.e. secular or religious.
- How will funeral expenses be met?

The type of funeral you choose will depend not only on the beliefs of the deceased, but also the wishes of those left behind. You may find it useful to sit down as a family and talk about what is important to each of you. The ultimate decision usually rests with the executor named in the will or, if there is no will, the nearest relative (also known as the administrator). However, it is often best to allow other family members to be involved, as this will help them with their own grieving process as well as providing support for the executor. If the deceased left a will, they may have specified their own preferences or may even have made their own arrangements, both of which might be a factor in your decision-making process. However, the executor has no legal obligation to carry out these wishes and can organise something different if they so wish.

While many people continue to choose a traditional funeral, it is now possible to opt for less formal or non-religious arrangements. For instance, you could choose to read a favourite poem, play a piece of music or have a 'green' burial with a special biodegradable coffin. This is your opportunity to say farewell in whatever way you and your family see fit. If you have a faith, your religious leader will be able to offer advice, suggestions and support. If not, your funeral director will be able to put you in touch with a humanist minister or help you arrange a secular ceremony.

The role of the funeral director

While it is possible to arrange a funeral without professional advice and help, most people engage the services of a funeral director. At a time when you are grieving, they can help with:

- Booking the venue for a service.

- Engaging a clergyman or conductor of services, according to your preference.

- Organising a cremation or burial, including ordering a coffin and finding a plot.

- Booking funeral cars and drivers.

- Providing a place for the body to rest until the funeral.

'The type of funeral you choose will depend not only on the beliefs of the deceased, but also the wishes of those left behind.'

- Arranging and accepting floral tributes, or arranging charitable donations if preferred.

- Placing a notice in the local newspaper.

There are a number of different ways you can go about finding a funeral director:

- Word of mouth from friends and family who have had good service.

- Ask for a list from the registrar when registering the death.

- If the deceased passed away in hospital, doctors and staff may be able to offer a recommendation.

- Look in the local telephone directory.

Most funeral directors in the UK are members of either the National Association of Funeral Directors (NAFD) or the Society of Allied and Independent Funeral Directors (SAIF). Members of either of these trade associations will offer you a price list on request and will not exceed any written price estimate without your permission. This will help you to stay within your agreed budget, giving you one less thing to worry about.

Funeral expenses

Firstly, it is important to check whether the deceased had a pre-paid funeral plan. If so, the final sum available will depend upon the amount paid in and the type of policy. It is worth checking with the deceased's solicitor (if they have one) to see if they are aware of any such scheme. Otherwise, checking through the personal documents of the deceased may provide details. If not, the next avenue to consider is the assets of the estate (the deceased person's finances) which might cover expenses. Sometimes money can be released in advance of settling the deceased's estate to cover these costs. You may also be able to negotiate a deferred bill or payment in instalments with the funeral director, who will take into account your individual circumstances. Where funds are not available from the deceased's estate or a pre-payment scheme, the person organising the funeral is liable, and can either choose to pay the bill themselves or can apply for government assistance towards burial, cremation or other associated costs. When registering the death, the registrar will be able to advise you on making an application to the government Social Fund.

Summing Up

What to do in the first week following the death of a loved-one:

- Register the death.
- Keep the death certificate in a safe place, as this will be needed over the coming weeks.
- Locate the will.
- Inform the deceased's place of work, GP and friends.
- Fill in the BD8 form and send to DWP.
- Engage a funeral director and begin making plans.

Chapter Two

The Estate and Finances

Once some of the more pressing tasks are completed, there are other matters to attend to. For some people, keeping busy can seem like a welcome relief from thinking about their loss. For others, organising finances can seem like an ordeal, making it difficult to cope. For this reason, it is important to ask for help from friends and family. Even if you are on your own, you can get support from a number of organisations (see help list).

Although this chapter is devoted to arranging the estate of the deceased, it begins by talking about you, and how you will manage during this time. You may need to take time off work or pay unexpected bills. If you have lost a partner, your income may suddenly be halved. It may seem heartless or mercenary to think about the effect of death upon your finances, but it is part of looking after yourself after suffering a bereavement.

Obtaining leave from work

Although it is not a legal entitlement for your employer to allow you a day off to attend a funeral, it is likely that your place of work will agree to your request, particularly if the deceased was a close relative or dependant. If, for some reason, your request is declined, you might decide to take the day as part of your holiday allowance. While there is not an official requirement to offer paid bereavement leave in the UK, many individual employers do operate their own scheme. Check with your manager or the head of human resources at your place of work. You may also need time away from work to settle the estate of the deceased person – even if it is simply a day to go through their personal belongings. Again, most employers will be sympathetic but it is vital to keep them informed, even if you find it difficult to speak about what has happened. Where more time off is needed, you may wish to organise an extended leave

'It may seem heartless or mercenary to think about the effect of death upon your finances, but it is part of looking after yourself after suffering a bereavement.'

of absence. The Citizen's Advice Bureau (CAB) is a free advisory body with a branch in every major town and city. The CAB will be able to inform you of your rights and help you to work through any employment-related problems.

Following bereavement, some people become very depressed and unable to cope with work. If this is the case, see your GP as soon as possible. They will be able to provide your employer with a report on your health which may form the basis of a claim for statutory sick pay. In any event, keep your employer informed as best you can. A friend or relative may be able to explain the situation on your behalf. To summarise:

- Check whether your place of work offers a bereavement leave scheme.

- Use your holiday allowance if necessary.

- See your GP as soon as possible if you find yourself too ill to return to work.

- Even if you are grieving, try to keep your employer informed as to whether you will be attending work.

Managing your finances

If bereavement drastically alters your financial situation, help is at hand. Surviving spouses and civil partners are entitled to a one-off bereavement payment of £2,000. This may help you to keep up with bills and other payments until you can rearrange your finances. If you are now the sole carer for your children, you may be entitled to additional support. Your local Jobcentre Plus will be able to advise you on the options available. If you have lost a child or someone for whom you were receiving benefits (such as a Carer's Allowance), contact the DWP as soon as you can to prevent overpayments which, if spent, you may struggle to pay back. Following bereavement, it may seem unimportant to think about money, but this is all part of taking care of yourself following a loss. Although it may be difficult, try not to allow bills to pile up as it's important to give yourself as little to worry about as possible during this difficult time.

Organising the estate

The estate is the name given to the belongings and financial assets of the deceased person. When someone dies, their property, investments and savings are distributed among those named in the will, minus legal fees and outstanding bills. The person who is named in the will to organise the estate is known as the executor. Where there is no will, the deceased person is said to have died intestate. In this instance, the role of organising the estate will fall to the nearest relative, and this person is known as the administrator. Since the processes are quite different, this section is divided into two parts.

Where there is no will (intestacy)

Sometimes the deceased person leaves no will, and this can prove difficult for those left behind. In this case, who organises the estate and those that benefit from it is determined by the rules of intestacy. The administrator (the person chosen to deal with the deceased person's finances) is the nearest natural relative. The following list shows the order in which priority is given.

- The spouse or civil partner of the deceased person. Unfair as it may seem, unmarried or co-habiting partners are not given priority and are not usually granted powers of administration.

- The children of the person who has died, or their grandchildren. Powers of administration will only be given where these descendants are over 18.

- The deceased person's parents will be chosen to administer the estate if none of the above apply.

- Where none of the above are alive, the deceased person's siblings (or their children) will be chosen. Siblings of 'whole blood' (i.e. sharing the same parents) are given priority over half-siblings.

- Next in the order of priority are the deceased's grandparents.

- The aunts and uncles of the deceased may be approached. Again, relatives of 'whole blood' will be given priority. If they are no longer living, their descendants will be chosen.

'Although it may be difficult, try not to allow bills to pile up as it's important to give yourself as little to worry about as possible during this difficult time.'

- Finally, the state or government (known as the 'Crown') will take over duties where no living relatives are available.

Where there is more than one possible administrator, the first person to apply for a grant of letters of administration will normally be chosen. If this cannot be agreed upon, then the case will need to be brought before the Probate Court. This process is complicated and best avoided. In the event that agreement cannot be reached, it will be necessary to engage a solicitor.

The role of the administrator

'Obtaining a grant of letters of administration will allow you access to bank and building society accounts belonging to the deceased person.'

In order to organise the estate, the administrator must apply for a grant of letters of administration from the Probate Registry (see help list). You can make this application through a solicitor, or personally. However, where the situation is complicated a solicitor can make the process of organising the estate easier. They can deal with banks, the DWP, unpaid bills and other matters on your behalf and will usually deduct their fee from the final amount of the estate. They will also be able to advise you on who should inherit and how much, and if any inheritance tax should be paid. Obtaining a grant of letters of administration will allow you access to bank and building society accounts belonging to the deceased person.

Whether you are the administrator (where no will is left) or the executor (where there is a will) you will need the following documents in order to deal with the estate:

- Bank and building society details to close accounts.
- Pension scheme documents.
- Details of shares/investment to be claimed.
- Mortgage/rental details so that landlords can be informed and property sold or bequeathed.
- Car and life insurance policy documents.
- Benefits or pension statements so policies can be cancelled.
- Loan and credit card statements.
- Utility and council tax bills to cancel and/or pay outstanding bills.

- Tax and wage details in order to pay outstanding debts or claim rebates.
- Property deeds/leases and keys to be sold or given to the beneficiary.
- Passport to return to the passport office.
- Driving licence and parking permits to return to the DVLA.
- TV/Internet provider details to cancel accounts.

If the deceased was self-employed, you will also need to find:

- Company accounts.
- Company registration documents.
- Tax and VAT returns details.

Who will inherit?

Where there is no will, all property and money will pass to the nearest relative (usually the deceased's spouse), along similar lines to the priority of administration. The exception to this is if property or accounts are held jointly – in this case, ownership will pass to the surviving owner.

Where there are children, the nearest relative will inherit up to £250,000. Half of any remainder will pass to the deceased's children and may be held in trust until they reach 18 years old. The other half will be held in trust and any interest is passed to the nearest relative during their lifetime. Upon their death, this remainder is passed to the surviving children.

In cases where the deceased had no children, the first £450,000 passes to the nearest relative (usually the spouse) and any remainder is passed to the parents of the deceased. If there are no parents living, brothers or sisters of the deceased (or their children) may inherit. In cases where there are no children or other relatives of 'whole blood' (as opposed to relations by marriage), the whole estate will pass to the spouse of the deceased.

In practice, these rules can prove complicated, so it is best to contact the CAB or a solicitor if in doubt. While co-habiting partners cannot inherit, it may be possible to make a claim on the estate. To do this, you'll need to prove that you were partly or wholly financially dependent upon the deceased.

If they left a will

When the person who has died has left a will, they will usually have named the person who is to be the executor. In order to begin to organise the estate, the executor will need to obtain a grant of probate in order to gain access to bank accounts and financial details of the person who has died. Where there is more than one executor, those named can either elect one person to apply for the grant of probate, or apply jointly. In order to attain the grant of probate, a number of forms must be filled in. These can be done alone although many people use a solicitor to ensure that legal matters are handled correctly. After this, the assets of the estate are distributed according to the wishes expressed in the will.

Summing Up

- The estate is the name given to the deceased person's belongings, which include any property owned along with their savings and assets.

- When someone dies, the estate needs to be organised. Any outstanding bills must be paid and the assets divided between those who are to inherit.

- A solicitor can help with this process and will charge a fee for their services.

- If the deceased person left a will, an executor will be named. It is their job to organise the estate.

- Where the person who died did not leave a will, the nearest relative will be named as administrator. It is their job to organise the estate.

Chapter Three

Shock, Numbness and Breaking Bad News

When someone dies, it is natural to feel numbness, shock or disbelief. You may find that you expect them to return at any moment, or struggle to accept the reality of what has happened. Immediately after someone dies you may also find yourself having to break bad news to others or help children to understand what has happened. These tasks can prove very difficult, especially if you yourself are struggling to comprehend the news. In this chapter we'll look at:

- What is meant by shock and how it affects both mind and body.

- How various rituals surrounding death can help us acknowledge what has happened.

- How to take care of yourself when you have received bad news.

- Ways of explaining death to children.

What is shock?

Following bereavement, shock can take many forms. You may have some of the following thoughts or feelings:

- He or she is going to walk through the door soon.

- This is just a bad dream.

- It must be a mistake!

- I'm fine.

- I don't understand what has happened.

You may also experience some of the following physical symptoms:

- Dizziness and nausea.
- Shakiness or weakness of the limbs.
- Faintness or light-headedness.
- Heaviness or excessive exhaustion.

After losing a loved one, many people report feeling as if they are in a bad dream and expect to wake up at any moment. This feeling of unreality is part of the experience of shock – often it takes time for our emotions to 'catch up' with what has happened. During the first days and weeks following bereavement, you may feel that you are 'going through the motions' or are watching events unfold from a distance – as if you were watching a film at the cinema. Some people say they feel fine as the bad news hasn't yet sunk in. For some people, shock manifests itself in a very physical way – they feel shaky, exhausted or faint. Sometimes, an initial feeling of unreality protects us from the realisation of what has happened. There is no time limit for how long this might last – for some people it may last a few days or weeks. For others, the realisation may take a number of months. Steph:

'When Jason died I just couldn't take it in. Sure, I heard the words but they didn't seem to mean anything. Everyone was crying and I just sat there. I wondered what was wrong with me.'

> 'After losing a loved one, many people report feeling as if they are in a bad dream and expect to wake up at any moment.'

This state of numbness can be frightening or disconcerting. Like Steph, you may watch others grieving around you and wonder why you don't feel the same. The important thing to remember is that you are not cold-hearted – there isn't anything wrong with you as a person. The effect of bereavement is different for everyone, and we each come to terms with loss in our own way. The feeling of numbness may persist for days or weeks and may come and go. As the months went by, Steph actually found numbness a comfort:

'I'd feel really devastated then go back to feeling numb again. Honestly it was a relief – if I felt that bad all the time I wouldn't have been able to go on.'

Some people have suggested that numbness and shock actually protect us from the full force of grief, meaning that the loss dawns upon us in stages rather than all at once. The important thing is to look after yourself as best you can, even when you are unable to do much else.

Taking care of yourself

When someone dies, it is easy to get caught up in all the things that need to be done. Alternatively, you may feel too stunned to do anything. In either case, it is easy to forget to look after your physical wellbeing. In the days following a terrible shock, you may feel too traumatised to eat properly, sleep or take any exercise. During this time it is common to experience headaches, shakiness, tiredness or heaviness in the limbs, since these are some of the ways our bodies register shock. Although it may seem unimportant at the moment, it is vital to keep as well as you can. Our mental and physical health is so closely interlinked that neglecting one can mean that the other suffers in the long run. If you can, try to:

- Eat every few hours, even if it is only a few bites of food at a time.

- Drink plenty of water – fruit juices are another option if you really can't face eating.

- Try to get outside once a day, even if it is to walk to the corner shop to buy milk or spending time in the garden.

- If you have nightmares or cannot sleep, try to catnap when you can – even if it is during the day.

- Breaking tasks into small steps and writing them down can help when your mind is stunned by loss.

While most bereaved people experience numbness following their loss, if you continue to feel nothing after months have passed it could be a sign that the loss is being repressed. When this happens, the bereaved person may refuse to acknowledge the reality of death in order to protect themselves from grief. While this is perfectly understandable, this may mean that all the devastating feelings are simply being saved up for later – a little like a pressure cooker. It is not uncommon for people to exhaust themselves by keeping busy to avoid feeling painful emotions. It may be months, or even years, down the line before grief catches up with them. It can be helpful to watch for danger signs, such as:

- Persistently refusing to acknowledge the loss.

- Keeping frantically busy.

- Carrying on as normal.

- Refusing to talk about the deceased.

- Turning down any/all offers of help.

Most bereaved people will show some of the behaviours above, so there is no hard and fast rule as to when numbness becomes a sign of repression. Nevertheless, try to bear the following points in mind:

- While it is important to try to keep a sense of routine and normality, it is also important to give yourself time to sit, think and digest the information.

- If you are able to, talking to others can be a great help at this time. It can be tempting to shut off or withdraw from others, but talking about death can help you to acknowledge and work through it.

- You may have been informed of the death by a family friend, relative, the police, hospital or a doctor. Chances are you will have heard the words, but they won't have gone in. Don't be afraid to ask questions, even if you have already been told the facts. Most healthcare professionals will understand that you are in shock and may need to have things explained again for the news to sink in. This is particularly true of children, who may ask the same things over and over again.

'In some cultures, thinking about death tends to be regarded as somewhat morbid. However, talking about what has happened allows us to acknowledge the loss and take the first step towards healing.'

Making sense of death

In some cultures, thinking about death tends to be regarded as somewhat morbid. However, talking about what has happened allows us to acknowledge the loss and take the first step towards healing. If you have been recently bereaved, you may find yourself:

- Talking continually about the circumstances of the death.

- Repeatedly describing the moment you were given the news.

- Asking to see the body again.

- Having recurrent dreams about the person who has died.

- Thinking about the last time you saw the deceased person.

These thoughts and feelings are perfectly natural and are part of trying to make sense of what has happened. You are still in a state of shock – and talking about the death or wanting to see the body is part of trying to grasp the reality of what has happened.

In our society, there are many practices and rituals which are used to mark the death of an individual. The following events are important because they help you to acknowledge the loss as well as to say goodbye:

- Giving away the deceased's belongings.
- The funeral service.
- Seeing the body at the chapel of rest or mortuary.
- Registering the death.
- The burial or cremation.

Shock is a natural response to bereavement even when it is someone elderly or ill that has died. Even if you have been caring for a terminally ill person, you may struggle to fully believe that they are gone. Even after the funeral has passed, it is normal to feel numb. Sometimes the reality of death will hit you afresh and will then subside into disbelief. This is part of the grieving process and the feelings of numbness and unreality will fade, though they can reappear for months or even years.

Breaking bad news

Just as adults feel numb and shocked following the death of a loved one, children also struggle to take in the fact that someone has died. Each child will react differently when given the bad news – one may become withdrawn while another may seem to continue as if nothing has happened. Here are some of the more common reactions from children who lose a loved one:

- They may become clingy as they fear that other relatives could die too.
- Sadly, they may be bullied or bully others. The latter is often an attempt to regain control.

- They may be exceptionally well-behaved, either to avoid further upsetting other bereaved relatives or in the hope that being 'good' will make the deceased person come back.

- They may regress to an early stage of development, such as thumb-sucking, bed wetting. etc.

There is no right or wrong response to loss, so it is important to let the child grieve in their own way. It may be hard, but try not to impose your idea of what 'healthy' grieving is upon them. A child may not cry and may even shock you by giggling or misbehaving at the funeral. It is important to remember that children release tension in different ways to adults.

'A child may not cry and may even shock you by giggling or misbehaving at the funeral. It is important to remember that children release tension in different ways to adults.'

Explaining to children about death

Since we have a natural instinct to protect children, we often try to soften the blow when it comes to breaking bad news. You might, for instance, tell them that a loved one has 'gone to sleep' or 'gone to heaven'. However, this can be confusing as the child infers that the person who has died has 'gone somewhere', and will therefore come back. Children have a literal way of understanding things, sometimes called 'magical' thinking. For instance, being told that a loved one has 'gone to sleep' may lead them to fear bedtime. They may also struggle with the idea of burial or cremation when, to their thinking, the person is simply asleep. By all means, share you own beliefs about what happens after death, but try to be as clear and direct about the reality of the situation as possible. Children often need to have things explained to them a number of times, and may keep asking the same questions. These questions may prove difficult to answer, but responding gently and consistently can help.

It may sound strange, but the truth can be preferable to some of the things a child might imagine. The death of a parent, for instance, can appear to the child as a punishment for not being 'good' enough. They may have absorbed disturbing pieces of information from the whispered conversations of adults, or may think that the person who has died simply chose to leave them. As well as allowing them to ask questions, it is often a good idea to ask them what they think has happened – this can open up discussion and help to correct distorted beliefs. Bill said:

'After her mum died, my daughter Andrea was trying so hard to be good. When I asked her how she felt, she replied that she had "been naughty, then Mummy went away". I had to explain that even if she had been angry with Mummy, angry feelings don't make people die. It was heart-breaking to realise she blamed herself and thought I might die too.'

It may seem natural to try to shield children from your own grief. However, although it can be upsetting for a child to see the adults around them being sad, it also gives out an important and positive message – that being sad is horrible, but it is okay and you can survive it.

'Children have a literal way of understanding things, sometimes called "magical" thinking. For instance, being told that a loved one has "gone to sleep" may lead them to fear bedtime.'

Summing Up

- Don't be afraid to ask questions about what has happened, even if things have been explained to you already.

- Try not to feel guilty about feeling numb – this is a natural response to a sudden shock and does not make you a bad person.

- Do try to share your feelings with others – keep talking!

- Allow yourself space and time to reflect, even when there are lots of things to do.

- Even if you feel 'fine' at first, don't try to accomplish too much on your own.

- Physical symptoms such as headaches and exhaustion are normal.

- Try not to take on any more than you have to, even if you are feeling for the moment that you can cope.

- Remember to take care of your physical wellbeing, even if you don't feel like eating or sleeping.

Just like adults, children can struggle to understand that a loved one is gone. You can help them through this difficult time by:

- Answering their questions honestly and openly, even when they are difficult.

- Explaining that they have not done anything wrong.

- Not hiding your grief from them, so that they know it is okay to be sad.

- Leaving the door open for further discussions.

- Informing school and their close friends as to what has happened.

Chapter Four

Anger and Guilt

When a loved one dies, it can seem as if you are on an emotional rollercoaster. You might feel numb, sad, devastated, tired or unable to sleep. However, there is one emotion that you may not expect to feel, and it can take you by surprise – anger. Even generally patient and laid back people can be shocked to find that they are absolutely furious. You may find yourself saying things like:

- Why did they (the deceased person) have to leave me?

- Didn't they know how difficult I would find life without them?

- They are selfish to leave us to cope!

- The hospital staff/doctor/place of work deserve to be punished.

The following chapter is aimed towards helping you to deal with these, completely natural, angry feelings.

Why so angry?

In cases where someone has died as a result of an accident or misdiagnosed illness, you may feel angry about the treatment they have received. Of course, in some cases this may be legitimate. There may well be a case for compensation or a genuine need for justice. However, sometimes we blame those around us simply because we feel angry towards the person who has left us. Where suicide is concerned, you may feel very angry towards the person for 'choosing' to leave you. In this way, anger is a response to perceived rejection. However, although the feeling might be overwhelming in cases of suicide, negligence or crime, anger is also a natural part of any bereavement – even where the deceased person had no choice in what happened to them.

Whatever the circumstances surrounding the death, many people feel guilty that they are angry. You might find yourself thinking:

- I must be a bad person for feeling angry.
- I know that they couldn't help what happened, so why am I angry?
- It is selfish to be angry.
- People will think I don't care about the deceased person.
- It's disrespectful to the deceased to be angry.

'Anger is a natural response to grief. It doesn't mean that you loved the deceased person any less – even if it feels that way in the heat of the moment.'

Anger is a natural response to grief. It doesn't mean that you loved the deceased person any less – even if it feels that way in the heat of the moment. Adrian says:

'It sounds awful, but when my mother died I was so angry with her. Deep down I knew that she couldn't help being ill, but I wished she had taken better care of herself. She was a very heavy smoker and I remember thinking at the time that she had chosen to smoke and have a shorter life at the expense of watching her grandchildren grow up. At the same time I felt guilty – I knew she had tried to give up so many times and she absolutely doted on the kids. Around that time one of my friends had started smoking again after going through a divorce. I was furious with her and told her that she was totally irresponsible and selfish. With hindsight, the person I was really angry with wasn't her, but Mum.'

Even when a relationship between two people has been strong and supportive, the person left behind is still likely to feel anger. Adrian had supported his mother through her illness, yet was surprised by how angry he felt when she died. It is important to remember that anger is a natural part of the grieving process. It may be irrational, misplaced or painful – but it is part of human nature.

Living with anger

Sometimes admitting that we are angry with the person who died is too difficult. Without even knowing it, you might begin to project these angry feelings elsewhere. For instance, you may:

38

- Shout or get easily frustrated with other people (as in Adrian's case).

- Lack patience.

- Become very angry over seemingly trivial matters.

- Blame others for the death (such as accusing hospital/care home staff, etc.).

It is not a coincidence that many family arguments and rifts between friends become more apparent after bereavement. Angry feelings begin to surface and are directed outwards or 'projected' onto others. It can be a horrible shock for an otherwise patient person (and those around them) to find themselves frustrated or even furious over seemingly trivial matters. From a young age, many of us are taught that anger is a dangerous and destructive emotion. However, it is an important part of the grieving process that cannot be ignored. In fact, the more you allow yourself to feel anger, the more quickly it is likely to disappear. Of course, that is not to say that it is a good idea to vent your anger on those around you (even if you may feel like it!), but you can certainly channel it into less destructive activities such as:

- Exercise – taking a very brisk walk around the block can help, as can some other high-energy activity such as vacuuming or cleaning.

- For some people, talking to the deceased person can help. Even if you do not believe that they can hear you, it can help to release tension.

- Listening to music can help to release strong feelings.

- Where your feelings might hurt others, talking to someone outside the family can help – particularly a counsellor or therapist who can listen without judgement.

- Writing a diary or letter can help to release tension. You needn't share it with anyone, and can destroy it after you have finished if you wish.

'From a young age, many of us are taught that anger is a dangerous and destructive emotion. However, it is an important part of the grieving process that cannot be ignored.'

Caring for an angry child

Just like adults, children may also struggle to manage angry feelings after someone they love has died. In the same way as adults, they may project their anger onto people and objects around them. A bereaved child may:

- Act aggressively towards other children at school.

- Be rude to teachers.

- Become quick to anger when they don't succeed at a task.

- Become hateful towards surviving family members.

Often, destructive behaviour is a way for a child to express painful feelings for which they have no other outlet. They may not have the words for the loss they have experienced and, just like adults, feel anger towards the person that has died for leaving them. When dealing with aggressive behaviour it can be useful to offer other ways for the child to express their emotions, such as:

- Storytelling – one idea is to ask the child to write or tell a story. You may be able to ask an older child to base it on how they are feeling, but you may find that even if you don't, the characters they invent will tell their story. Alternatively, you could read them a story. There are many books on the market written for children that deal indirectly with loss.

- Art – most children like to paint, draw or make things, so encourage them to be creative. Try not to worry about the mess or the final piece of work – the important thing is for them to release tension.

- Offer a 'cool down' zone – giving children an area to cool down, reflect or have time out when they are feeling angry can help them to manage their own feelings.

'Often, destructive behaviour is a way for a child to express painful feelings for which they have no other outlet.'

Finally, if it is at all possible, try to encourage children to voice their feelings. While really destructive behaviour can't go unchecked, do try to talk to them about what has made them angry rather than punishing them. Of course, many of these activities are also suitable for adults who are struggling to cope with anger following the death of a loved one. Immersing yourself in art work (it doesn't need to be a masterpiece) can provide an outlet for anger.

If only I had. . .

As well as feeling guilty about being angry, it is common for people to feel a deep sense of regret that they didn't 'do more' for the person who has died.

My experience:

On the Easter weekend before my uncle died, my family had a get together. Unfortunately, I arrived late and missed him and his girlfriend by an hour. After I heard that he had died, I wished that I had just got there a little earlier to see him one last time. I still have the Easter card he left for me, but it took a long time for me to stop feeling guilty about not seeing him that day.

In my case, there was no way I could have known what was going to happen, yet I still felt tormented by the fact that I missed out on that last chance to see him. This is a common experience for many survivors of bereavement, who feel that there was something they could/should have done or said with the benefit of hindsight. It is not unusual to become almost fixated on the final words, visit or contact that you had with the person who has died. You may have some of the following thoughts and feelings:

- They didn't know that I loved them.
- They died feeling angry with me.
- There were so many things I should have said.
- I should have known that they were going to die!
- I should have visited/called/spent time with them more frequently.

Almost every bereaved person feels regret about things they 'should' have done, but it is important to remember that in many (perhaps even most) relationships, many things remain unspoken. This is not to say that the person who has died didn't know how you felt about them. In my case, the fact that I wasn't able to see my uncle one last time didn't detract from all the time that we had spent together. Adele had a similar experience:

'On the morning before his accident, James left for work really early. We'd had a row the night before – nothing serious, just bickering. I can't get over the fact that the last words we exchanged were in anger.'

In Adele's case, what haunted her was the idea that James left the house thinking that she didn't love him. Again, this is something that many people struggle with following the death of a loved one. If you parted from the person on less-than good terms, it can be hard not to dwell on past mistakes.

'As well as feeling guilty about being angry, it is common for people to feel a deep sense of regret that they didn't "do more" for the person who has died.'

Letting go of guilt

As we've said, guilt is a very painful emotion. There are, however, practical things you can do to lessen its power:

- Try to remember the whole of your relationship with the person who has died, rather than focusing on what you did or didn't say the last time you saw them.

- Sometimes it can help to imagine what the deceased person would say to you when you are feeling bad – would they want you to feel guilty?

Summing Up

- Anger is a common and natural response to loss.

- Allowing yourself to feel anger is likely to make the feeling abate more quickly.

- For both adults and children, it can help to find a productive (rather than destructive) outlet for anger.

- Almost everyone who is bereaved regrets something they did or said before a loved one's death. This is normal and a very natural response to loss.

- It is important to look at your relationship with the deceased person as a whole, rather than selectively remembering what went wrong.

- Try to be kind to yourself – it is unlikely that the person who has died would want you to feel guilty.

Chapter Five

Sadness and Grief

When someone you love has died, it is natural to feel intense sadness as well as a longing to be with them again. These feelings are not purely psychological, as you may feel the loss in your body as well as your mind. Ryan says:

'The sadness was dragging me down all the time. I had moments when I missed him so much I could feel it to the pit of my stomach.'

As Ryan discovered, grief can seem to saturate your whole being and is one of the most painful emotions a human being can face. That said, it is important to remember that you can survive and get through it, even if, for the moment, the future feels hopeless. This chapter looks at why we grieve as well as practical and emotional strategies to cope with sadness.

How long will I feel like this?

Grief can last for many years, although it is liable to be more intense in the first 18 months. Sometimes, however, sadness can take us by surprise years after the event, particularly when something reminds us of the person we have lost. In cases where a loss was never really mourned, it can take years for sadness to evolve. For instance, people who have lost a parent as a very young child may suddenly find themselves grieving the loss when they are older, particularly after they have had their own children. Sophie says:

'My mother died when I was a little girl, but her death was never really talked about. My family thought I was too young to go to the funeral, so life just carried on. I remember feeling confused, but I still played with my friends and went to school. When I had a daughter in my late 20s, it just sort of hit me…I realised what I had missed out on and I couldn't stop crying.'

There is no specific timescale or length of time that is 'okay' to feel sad. The way you react to a loss will be different to other people. The important thing to remember is that you can move forwards with the right support and care – and this also means caring for yourself. For most people, it is not a case of 'getting over' a bereavement, but learning to live with it. The sadness may never vanish, but it will slowly diminish over time. In this country, crying or appearing visibly upset is somewhat stigmatised. In particular, men may find it more difficult to grieve openly due to the expectation that they should be somehow 'strong' or have a 'stiff upper lip'. In many cultures, however, mourners at a funeral will be more vocal about their grief. Sometimes then, we need reminding that it is okay to cry, and that this is a natural response to loss.

Coping with loss

'Feelings of intense sadness tend to begin when the death of a loved one becomes "real".'

Feelings of intense sadness tend to begin when the death of a loved one becomes 'real'. For some people this happens at the funeral, for others it may be registering the death. Sometimes, however, it can be sparked off by something seemingly unrelated, as in Terri's case:

'I'd always been close to my father, but when he died everyone (including me) was surprised at how well I coped. Six months later I was in a garden centre with my partner choosing plants. It suddenly hit me that I would never visit Dad again on a Sunday to help with his garden. I was so upset that my partner had to help me into the car and take me home.'

As Terri found, it is often the case that grief seems to hit us when we are least prepared for it. Some people seem to be coping very well, particularly during the time that they are receiving support from friends and family. However, it is often later down the line that the sadness and the longing to be with the person who has died can really take hold. At times like this, there are things you can do that may help, although what is effective for one person may not be for another. It is therefore a case of finding what works for you. In the past it was considered that grief was a process by which we sever ties with the dead person. However, these days it is recognised that maintaining emotional links with a lost loved one can actually help. For instance, some people may find it comforting to visit the grave or talk to the deceased person. This needn't be taken as a sign that the bereaved person is in denial – simply that this is what helps them at this stage of their grief.

Out and about

If you are feeling very low, it is easy to convince yourself that friends or family won't want to see you or find you a 'burden'. Often this has more to do with the way in which you perceive yourself, rather than what they actually feel. For some people, being asked 'how are you?' or talking about the person who has died may be too much to bear. Understandably, people want to know how you are feeling and may ask questions – but if you don't want to talk about it, don't feel pressured into doing so. Most people will take your feelings on board if you explain that you need a break from talking about your loss. The important thing is that you keep talking with others, even if the topic of conversation has nothing to do with bereavement. It may seem impossible to keep socialising as all you may want to do is shut yourself away, but there are some things you can do to make it easier:

- Explain to friends that you'd like to drop by their house for a very quick visit – that way you can leave if and when you feel you'd like to be alone.

- If talking is too hard, meet a friend for swimming, shopping or the cinema. The distraction may provide welcome relief from thinking about your loss.

- Explain to friends that you can only stay out for half an hour or so – there's no need to commit yourself to a whole day out if you don't feel ready.

Sometimes, however, you may be dismayed to find that people begin to avoid you. They may not know what to do or say and may be afraid that they will upset you or somehow make things worse. This can be very painful, as Maria found out:

'A few days after my baby Jack died I saw one of my friends in town. She'd sent me a message after hearing the news, but I hadn't seen her. I was going to walk over and speak to her, but to my surprise she ducked into a nearby shop. I knew that she saw me and was trying to pretend she hadn't – it was really hurtful. A few weeks later she wrote me a letter and apologised. She said she was really ashamed of herself.'

'If you are feeling very low, it is easy to convince yourself that friends or family won't want to see you, or find you a "burden". Often this has more to do with the way in which you perceive yourself, rather than what they actually feel.'

When friends act in what seems to be a surprisingly callous way, it can be difficult to forgive. It's easy to say that bereavement brings out people's true colours – and in some cases it is true – but this is not always the full picture. When someone suffers a profound loss, their friends or family may feel inadequate and helpless and are simply afraid of making things worse. They may also feel that anything they say will somehow be wrong or tactless. After losing his fiancée, Mark experienced a similar reaction from his colleagues:

'I noticed that everyone was being very careful around me – which made me feel awkward. I just wanted to be treated normally, but it would go quiet when I walked into the office. After a while I spoke to one of my workmates – he said that people didn't want to upset me by speaking about their weekend plans. He also told me that one of my colleagues was engaged. I'd be lying if I said that it didn't remind me of what I had lost, but I was so pleased for her and her boyfriend. I was relieved when my colleague spoke to others in the office for me. He told them they didn't have to tiptoe around me.'

In Mark's case, being upfront about what he needed from his colleagues was effective. Worried they would hurt him by behaving normally, they withdrew from him which actually caused him more pain. Sometimes people may need to know what you need (or don't, as the case may be) from them.

Remember happy times

Sometimes when someone dies the focus can often move from their life to how they died. Where death was a result of violence or suicide, the circumstances surrounding the death can seem all-consuming. Although it is very difficult when you are sad, recalling happier times or other aspects of the person's life can offer some comfort. For instance, you might like to start a 'memory book' with photographs, old train tickets or letters to remind you of days out or time spent together. Alternatively, you could pick a particularly special day or occasion and write about it. However, if the emotions you are experiencing are too raw, it may take a while before you are able to look at old photographs. Don't feel that you have to do any of the activities suggested – everyone grieves in their own way. Again, it's a case of finding activities or ways of remembering that offer you some comfort – whatever stage you are at in your grief.

Build your self-esteem

When someone dies, life can seem to have no meaning. Often our sense of identity is bound up with the people closest to us, so that when they are gone we can lose our sense of who we are. For Jessica, the loss of her husband made her feel that it simply wasn't worth going on:

'John always did everything. He was really organised and managed to keep our finances in check. His friends almost adopted me, so I let him become my whole world. When he died last spring, I felt totally lost – I felt like I was nothing without him. There seemed to be no point in going on. I know he'd want me to be happy, because he always believed in me. It's been hard but a year later, I'm slowly building a new life and am finding things about myself that I never knew before.'

Having low self-esteem can make the grieving process even harder, as you may feel that you don't 'deserve' to be happy because someone you loved has died. When a close relationship has been ended by bereavement, you may also start to think about your own identity as an individual. After the devastation of losing her husband, Jessica started to live 'for herself'. This meant finding out what she enjoyed and shaping a new identity. If you have been recently bereaved, this type of thinking may seem a million miles away. There are, however, small things that you can do on a day-to-day basis to help you learn to value yourself:

'Often our sense of identity is bound up with the people closest to us, so that when they are gone we can lose our sense of who we are.'

- Every day write down at least two things you have managed to accomplish – even if they are 'minor' things, like taking the dog for a walk or going shopping. It can be reassuring to know that you are still a capable person.

- Give yourself little rewards for accomplishing things – simple pick-me-ups such as a long bath, or perhaps cooking yourself a nice meal.

- Try something new – whether this is a hobby, an evening class or volunteering. As well as a good way to meet new people, you will start to develop your own interests.

- Even when you have lots of things to do, or are feeling very low, try to spend at least 30 minutes a day doing something enjoyable – even if it's just watching a favourite soap or reading a book.

■ Finally, be gentle with yourself. When you are feeling guilty or sad, try to imagine what you would say to a friend in the same position – often we are harder on ourselves than we would be on anyone else!

Complicated grief

There are a number of factors that can complicate the process of grieving. If you were estranged from the person who has died, there may be a sense of unfinished business. This can make it hard to come to terms with the loss and you may feel that you don't have the 'right' to grieve. Low self-esteem can also complicate matters, as well as situations where the relationship is not publicly acknowledged – for instance in gay relationships where the family were not aware of the deceased person's sexual orientation. Similarly, the relationship might have taken the form of an affair or kept secret from work colleagues where relationships between staff members were frowned upon. In any of these situations, bereavement can leave you feeling isolated. Without support it can be difficult to work through the process of mourning, especially since those around you may not know what is wrong. Sam says:

'My brother and I had never really had a good relationship and were estranged from each other for a year before he died. I felt that I didn't have any right to be sad because of the way we had argued.'

Where the relationship was strained it is important to remember that it is okay to feel sad, even if you were not in contact at the time the person died. In a way, you are also mourning the loss of the relationship you had hoped to have. In order to move forward, it is often important to make your peace with the person who has died. Perhaps you could write a letter to the person who has died, explaining how you felt and why you acted in the way that you did. It is not necessary to share the contents with anyone else if you choose not to – the aim is to help you come to terms with what has happened. Where a relationship was unacknowledged by others, you might choose to have your own memorial service, perhaps inviting close friends who knew about the relationship. Chapter 9 looks at other specific types of grief including bereavement by suicide and accidental death.

Grief or depression?

Depression is an illness characterised by low mood and tiredness. It is a condition which requires medical attention and can be treated by psychotherapy, medication and lifestyle changes. If you have recently been bereaved it is natural that you will feel sad, but if you are really struggling with everyday life it is often worth visiting your GP to rule out underlying depression. The symptoms of depression are very similar to those experienced in grief. These include:

- Loss of appetite or desire for excessive overeating.

- Disturbed sleep pattern.

- Loss of interest in sex.

- Low mood.

- Suicidal thoughts.

- Tearfulness.

- Desire to withdraw from others.

- Loss of ability to concentrate.

However, there is one important difference: grief is a process that people move through – even if it takes a long time and is very painful. Depression, on the other hand, is something which does not (usually) resolve itself and is marked by a persistently low mood. With grieving, the symptoms listed can be seen to relate to a profound loss. With depression, however, low mood can come out of the blue. Alternatively, it may surface if the grieving period continues for a very long time. Sometimes depression can be triggered by a loss in the past which was not mourned at the time. This is particularly likely if the original bereavement happened during childhood. A relatively trivial event, such as a change of job, house or a neighbour moving house may trigger depression as some feelings from this original unmourned loss begin to surface. Alternatively, a profound loss can trigger depression as you struggle to find your way through your grief. If you were already mildly depressed before the bereavement, the loss may exacerbate the existing condition. In either case, you needn't suffer in silence. There are things you can do:

'Grief is a process that people move through – even if it takes a long time and is very painful. Depression, on the other hand, is something which does not (usually) resolve itself and is marked by a persistently low mood.'

- Visit your GP. They will ask you a number of questions to establish whether your low mood is down to grief or long term or acute depression.

- If you are prescribed any medication, take it according to the instructions.

- Talk! There are many organisations who are able to give advice and simply listen (see help list).

Finally, if you are feeling suicidal you must speak to a professional at once. Whether you visit A&E, your GP or phone the Samaritans, there are people out there who can help you – let them.

Longing and searching

As well as sadness, bereaved individuals usually experience a deep longing for the deceased person and may engage in what some psychologists call 'searching'. If you lose someone you love, you may find yourself drawn to places where you expect them to be. It is not unusual for bereaved people to 'see' the person who has died or to hear their voice. If you have been bereaved you may:

- Have dreams of the deceased person which are very vivid.

- Think you see them in a crowd or walking down the street.

- Believe that you have heard them speak.

- Find yourself wandering around aimlessly as if looking for the person you have lost.

For many people, these experiences can be very frightening. It can be upsetting to 'see' the person you have lost and you may even worry that you are going mad. In fact, these experiences are very common amongst bereaved people, and are often the result of the deep yearning to see the deceased person again. For people with religious or spiritual beliefs, these experiences may be interpreted as evidence that the person is still with them in some way, and may afford some comfort. Either way, it is important to remember that such incidences are very rarely associated with a serious mental health condition and are usually just another (albeit strange and often distressing) way that the mind responds to loss.

Summing Up

▪ There is no set timescale for grieving. The nature of the relationship, availability of support and your self-esteem are all factors in the length and intensity of mourning.

▪ Grieving may not begin until days, weeks or months after the death.

▪ Talking to and being with others can help, even if the conversation isn't about the person who has died.

▪ It may sound clichéd but it is helpful to focus on the life of the person, rather than the manner of their death.

▪ You may not feel that you deserve to be happy, but learning to value yourself is an important step towards moving forward.

▪ If your relationship with the deceased was unacknowledged or strained, you may need extra support.

▪ It is important to check that you are not becoming overly tired, run-down or depressed. A visit to your GP will help you to keep on top of your health.

▪ Seeing or hearing the deceased person is not an unusual response to grief – it doesn't mean that you are going mad.

▪ If you feel suicidal it is vital to talk to someone – you don't have to suffer alone.

▪ For more information on depression, see *Depression – The Essential Guide* (Need2Know).

Chapter Six

Acceptance and Moving Forwards

If you have recently been bereaved, acceptance can seem a million miles away, but much further down the line you may notice that you have begun to adjust to the absence of a loved one. Acceptance is not something that suddenly happens, but a gradual process which takes place over a number of months or years. So, what is meant by acceptance? Firstly, it does not mean forgetting the person who has died. Secondly, acceptance is not simply 'getting over it.' What is meant by acceptance is usually that the bereaved person has learned to live with the loss. Here are some things that different people mean by acceptance:

- Not expecting the person who has died to walk through the door at any moment.

- Realising that there was nothing that could be done to prevent them from dying.

- Being able to remember the person's life rather than their death.

- Altering your life in a way that takes into account their absence.

- Looking back and remembering something positive about their life without being overwhelmed by sadness.

- Talking about the deceased person in the past tense (e.g. Jack was a great joker, rather than 'is' a great joker).

What is meant by acceptance will vary from person to person. For Sarah it meant finally realising that the person who died was gone forever:

'Acceptance is not something that suddenly happens, but a gradual process which takes place over a number of months or years.'

'For about a year after he died, I still expected Grandad to walk through the door and greet the kids with his usual smile. It was as if he was on holiday and I expected him to come back. After about 18 months, I found that I had stopped expecting him on a Sunday. In my head I knew all the time that he wouldn't come back – but it took a year and a half for my heart to catch up.'

For Emma, acceptance was finally being able to think about the life of her brother, rather than the way he died:

'When Danny died it was almost like I couldn't think of anything apart from the way he died. It was as if his suicide had totally blotted him out as a person. I was full of guilt, regret and anger and I kept reliving that awful day again and again. It's so hard, but I know he wouldn't want to be remembered this way. It's been a long road, but I can now look back at some of the great things he did without dwelling just on his suicide.'

Acceptance is not a linear process. In other words, we don't move through the stages of grief to achieve it in a straightforward way. You might, for instance, feel a sense of acceptance one day, only to find yourself angry and disbelieving the next. You may, however, find that the days spent in a state of intense grief become lessened over time until, eventually, the days you feel okay come to outweigh the bad times. Sometimes, realising that you have come to live with the loss of a loved one can bring on a fresh bout of sadness or anger. We can see then that the idea of acceptance is more complicated than simply 'feeling better.'

Fear of forgetting

The process of accepting a loss is often complicated by the fact that it feels like we are shutting out the person who has died. Months down the line, you may catch yourself humming a tune or having a laugh. The first time that this happens can be quite horrifying, as Donal remembers:

'About a year after my teenage daughter died, I remember I was watching something on television. The presenter made a really funny quip which made me roar with laughter. Then I suddenly realised what I had done and felt ashamed. I thought "what sort of a father must I be to forget Sarah after a year?"'

Allowing yourself to enjoy life does not mean that you have forgotten the person who has died or that you have stopped caring about them. It is easy to feel that you have done the deceased person a disservice by moving on, but it is worth considering what you would say to them if the roles were reversed. If you were the one who had died, wouldn't you want them to find some enjoyment in life? For this reason it is important to give yourself 'permission' to feel enjoyment again. If every minute of every day was spent grieving and remembering (as it often is in the first few months following a bereavement) it would be more than any human being could bear.

Dealing with other people's expectations

After about six months, you may find that some people have an expectation that you will be largely coping and will have moved on with your life. It can be hard to be flooded with sympathy and offers of help, only to have them vanish a few months down the line. While some people (often those who have experienced bereavement themselves) will still remain sympathetic, there are always those who suppose that just because you are outwardly coping, or more time has passed, then you must be almost 'back to normal'. Many of us are adept at hiding our emotions from others. Unfortunately, if your disguise is too effective you may find people thinking that you really are fine. This can be difficult to cope with, particularly if they make unthinking comments or jokes, or your work colleagues expect you to function at the same rate that you did before the bereavement. In these cases, it is often wise to let them know what they can realistically expect from you – sometimes a gentle reminder is needed. Communication is key here, whether you talk to friends, family, work colleagues or even a psychotherapist. Keeping things bottled up in order to keep others happy can be an exhausting and self-defeating strategy.

Alternatively, there may be people who cannot understand, or may even be angry that you are able to cope. This is most likely to happen in cases of shared grief where one person seems to reach acceptance more quickly than another. David:

'Christa's parents were angry when I seemed to be coping after she died. I had been her carer for years and had watched as her health gradually deteriorated. I had done all my crying in the years I looked after her, so when she passed

'Allowing yourself to enjoy life does not mean that you have forgotten the person that has died or that you have stopped caring about them.'

away I felt relieved that she didn't have to suffer anymore. When I said as much, her father took it very badly. He wanted her to keep fighting and wasn't ready to say goodbye.'

David's experience isn't unusual – someone who is grieving is in the grip of very strong emotions and can find it hard to understand that others may feel differently. This is one of the reasons why close relationships can become strained following bereavement. It is important to remember that people grieve in different ways and over different timescales.

Your life without them

'Initially, it may be useful to compile a list of tasks to be completed. This will not only give you a sense of control, but can also help you to prioritise what is important.'

When you lose someone close to you, it can seem as if there is no point to anything. When your life has revolved around them, it can be difficult to see what is left for you. However, as you begin to accept the loss you may start to think about your own future – and feel guilty for doing so. The important thing to remember is that you aren't forgetting them, but are doing what you need to do in order to move forwards with your own life. When someone close to us dies, we often realise the role that they played in everyday life. In close relationships we often fall into certain habits or roles. For instance, your partner may have taken care of household bills or a parent may have looked after the children after school. These practical tasks may become difficult after the person's death, and can often add to the burden of grief you experience. It can therefore be helpful to reassess your day-to-day life to ensure that various jobs or chores don't build up. This may mean learning a new skill or finding outside support to help you cope. Initially, it may be useful to compile a list of tasks to be completed. This will not only give you a sense of control, but can also help you to prioritise what is important. Try dividing tasks to be completed into separate areas such as:

- Bills, paperwork and finances.
- Cleaning and laundry.
- DIY jobs, household repairs.
- Car maintenance.
- Cooking.

- Shopping.
- Childcare.
- Leisure time.

Each section can then be further broken down into particular jobs, such as sorting out car insurance, vacuuming or making the children's lunches. Where the deceased person had a role to play, try to think of other alternatives. Consider whether you can complete the job yourself. If not, who could help? Maybe the children could lend a hand with small chores such as the dusting. Perhaps you'll need to ask someone's advice about finances or find a mechanic for car repairs. It is also useful to draw up a schedule to plan your week. It is vitally important not to try to accomplish too much in the months following bereavement when you are likely to be feeling exhausted, emotional and vulnerable. Conversely, completing small jobs and feeling organised can help to gain a sense of control and will prevent you from becoming overwhelmed. Whether the deceased person played a very practical role in your life or not, restructuring your life is a key step in coming to terms with the loss and helping yourself to stay on top of things during a difficult time.

What next?

It is important to remember that acceptance isn't final. You may be having a good day, week or even year but something will happen to make you feel that you are right back to square one. This is natural, although it is easy to feel disheartened. Don't be afraid to continue to ask for help and support when you are struggling – even if it is months or years down the line. Even if you are feeling okay, try not to make big decisions or put yourself under pressure in the year following the death of a loved one. There may be times when you need to go back to coping with things day-by-day. Most importantly – take care of yourself.

Summing Up

- Accepting the fact that a loved one is dead is not the same as forgetting them or 'getting over it'.

- It is natural to feel guilty when you begin to find some enjoyment in life again. Allowing yourself to laugh or do something you enjoy doesn't mean you are being disrespectful or uncaring towards the deceased person.

- Other people may expect you to cope or feel 'better' before you are ready. Telling other people how you are really feeling can help them understand.

- People grieve over different timescales and in different ways. Sometimes this can lead to conflict.

- It can be particularly tough to cope when the deceased person performed set roles in your everyday life. It can be useful to reassess your day-to-day tasks in order to prevent you from becoming overwhelmed.

Chapter Seven

Anniversaries, Birthdays and Planning Ahead

Even as everyday life seems manageable again, it is natural that certain memories about the person who has died will crop up – sometimes most unexpectedly. Rather than viewing these sad moments as a set-back, try to see them in context of your general ability to cope. Many bereaved people report that the first anniversary of the death or first family celebration without a loved one is the hardest, since they don't occupy a familiar seat or role. However, for a number of years to come it is likely to be difficult on certain days and certain occasions. There are many steps you can take to make these days easier. This chapter looks at coping with these occasions and finding positive ways to remember the person who has died.

Coping with family occasions

When families gather together to celebrate, the absence of the person who has died can seem even more apparent. Some people, therefore, opt to cancel such plans. However, being on your own at a time like Christmas can prove even harder, as it throws into sharper relief what has been lost. In cases where other family members would normally attend, it may actually prove easier to be together – especially if you have suffered the same loss and can therefore support each other. The first family occasion following the loss of a loved one may be a somewhat sombre affair, but will usually become easier as each year passes. Maintaining some familiarity is particularly important for children, even if the preparations seem like a chore. While a family occasion may be somewhat sad, it can allow a child to see that life does go on and it is still okay for them to have fun, even if they miss the deceased person terribly.

'The first family occasion following the loss of a loved one may be a somewhat sombre affair, but will usually become easier as each year passes.'

That said, for the first year following a bereavement it can sometimes help to change the familiar arrangements. Perhaps you and your family could stay with a friend or the other side of the family. It can also help to plan between you what each person can do to help. If it was the deceased person's job to cook the dinner, perhaps you could all chip in to make different parts of the meal. Or if that is too much, why not break with tradition and go out for lunch, to somewhere new. This can provide a welcome relief from your familiar environment with its sad memories.

Remembering with children

People often assume that it is 'unhealthy' for children to dwell on a lost loved one. Chances are, children will remember anyway and will pick up on the atmosphere during the anniversary of the death or birthday. Unfortunately, this often teaches them that such matters are 'not to be talked about' or that speaking about the deceased person is somehow taboo. In fact, it can be helpful for children to have somewhere to go if they are feeling sad, or a place to visit when they want to remember. This doesn't have to be the grave or formal memorial stone – it can be a place that reminds them of the person who has died. Here are some ideas:

- Create a special space in the garden to remind them of the person who has died. Children can help to plant and choose the flowers as a way of doing something constructive. Be sure that they are involved and that there is no pressure on them to get the planting 'right' – allow them to have free reign and it will be their place which they can turn to when they are feeling sad or thoughtful.

- Perhaps there is a special book or a place in the home that they can turn to whenever they want to think about the person who has died.

- When an anniversary is approaching that might be difficult, let them know they have someone to talk to. You could speak to the teacher and let them know that your child is likely to be having a difficult time. Tell the child that the teacher is there to speak to whenever and if they need to. Even if the child chooses not to mention it to the teacher it may help them to know that there is someone sympathetic nearby if they need them.

- Finally, it is worth bearing in mind that children may remember things in a different way to adults. Just because they don't want to join in with a memorial service or visit the grave doesn't mean they don't care – they may have other ways of remembering.

Holidays

The annual break from work can be a difficult time for people who have been bereaved, especially if the part of the year was previously spent in the company of the person who has died. Often planning a trip abroad can occupy people for a long time, acting as a welcome relief from the burdens of work. Margaret:

'Every year Pete and I would go to our villa in Italy – it was our little getaway and we always had a great time. After he died I couldn't bear the thought of going there alone, so I let it out to another couple. I wasn't going to have a holiday at all but my friend convinced me to go with her – to Iceland of all places! It was completely different – and bracingly cold! Pete would have hated it and, somehow, that made it easier to cope.'

If you are used to planning alongside the person that has died, it can take the pleasure out of it. As Margaret found, making alternative arrangements or doing something different can help. Here are some suggestions:

- Some organisations offer holidays for bereaved people or lone parents. There are a number of organisations listed in the help list.

- Perhaps you could go away with another friend or family member, even if it is for a shorter break.

- You might decide to go somewhere completely different, or do something out of character. Where have you always wanted to go?

- You could join a travel group. For the lone traveller, a travel group can provide a structure, itinerary, company and most importantly – a good laugh!

'Children may remember things in a different way to adults. Just because they don't want to join in with a memorial service or visit the grave doesn't mean they don't care – they may have different ways of remembering.'

Coping with difficult days at work

In the first few years following a bereavement, many people worry how they will cope at work on anniversaries and birthdays. You may not be so close to your work colleagues as you are to friends and family, making it more difficult to share your feelings. Perhaps you are anxious to appear capable and focused and are worried about seeming unprofessional. However, it is worth remembering that the majority of people will experience bereavement during the course of their working lives, so there is a good chance that there are others in your workplace who will be able to understand how you are feeling.

If your job requires you to be on top form all the time, you might choose to take significant days (such as a loved one's birthday or the anniversary of their death) as holiday from work. However, only you can be the judge as to whether this will prove beneficial. It can be easy to slip into despair if you spend the day alone. You could, therefore, arrange something else on that day – perhaps meeting with friends who also knew the deceased person and are likely to be supportive. Alternatively, you might be certain that a day to reflect and think is just what you need. For some, keeping busy is an important part of coping during difficult anniversaries, so you may decide to go into work as normal and keep to yourself. Another option is to inform colleagues in advance that you may struggle a little on certain days as this might prevent them from overburdening you with work. Whichever way works best for you, planning in advance can help you to feel prepared and supported.

'It is worth remembering that the majority of people will experience bereavement during the course of their working lives, so there is a good chance that there are others in your workplace who will be able to understand how you are feeling.'

Summing Up

■ Anniversaries and birthdays can prove particularly difficult following a bereavement. Planning in advance can help you to cope.

■ It is natural to struggle with difficult emotions on these days – it doesn't necessarily mean that you have taken a step backwards.

■ On occasions usually spent with the person that has died it can help to arrange a different activity.

■ Children can find it helpful to have somewhere to remember the person that has died.

■ Holidays can be a testing time if you are used to spending them with the deceased person. Again, making alternative arrangements can prove a welcome distraction.

■ If an anniversary falls on a working day, it can help to let colleagues know the situation.

Chapter Eight

Supporting Someone Who is Bereaved

When a friend, relative or work colleague suffers a bereavement, it can be difficult to know what to do for the best. You may feel that you want to support them but don't know how to go about it. Perhaps their loss brings back difficult feelings from bereavements you have suffered in the past. People fear that they will do or say the 'wrong thing' and make someone's grief even more painful. If someone close to you experiences bereavement, you may feel:

- Helpless.

- Overwhelmed.

- Embarrassed and awkward.

- Inadequate.

- Frustrated.

It is important to remember that all of these feelings are natural and may change over time. The way you react will also depend on the nature of the relationship. If the bereaved person is a parent, it can be difficult to find your roles suddenly reversed as you have to care and support them. If the bereaved person is a close friend, you might find that your relationship seems strained, or that you start to examine yourself as a friend. Whoever you are supporting, it is natural to feel helpless, and it can be very painful to see someone you care about in deep distress. As a result of feeling inadequate or helpless, people often distance themselves from the person who has suffered a loss. This, however, can be very painful for the bereaved person, who may see this as a rejection or lack of concern.

Showing that you care

Aside from listening and being supportive, there are other practical things that people often do when someone they know has been recently bereaved. These include:

- Sending a card – 'with sympathy' or 'thinking of you' cards can help you to find the words if you're not sure what to say. A few lines to say that your thoughts are with them and their family can help to make the message more personal.

- Sending a letter – depending on your relationship with the bereaved person, you may choose to write a letter. This can be more personal for the recipient, and may be appropriate to send to a close friend who you can't visit in person.

- Sending flowers and/or a donation – people often like to send flowers to the funeral, even if they are unable to attend. Before doing so, it is a good idea to check whether the deceased's family are accepting floral tributes. Some families prefer to arrange their own flowers and ask people to donate to a charity in the deceased person's name.

How can I help?

Adam: 'When my partner died, all my friends said if there was anything I needed I should ask them, but I found it so difficult to ask – I didn't want to put them to trouble. In the weeks and months following Simon's death, I was so lonely and needed help with sorting out our joint finances. One of my friends said "I can go through paperwork and I've got the weekend free. Let me know what you need me to do." It was such a relief, because I knew he meant it, and wasn't just being polite.'

Offering to help with practical things such as shopping, cooking or housework can be helpful to someone who has been recently bereaved. As Adam discovered, most people will offer general help, but sometimes people feel as if they are a burden and may therefore be reluctant to take up the offer. When asked if they would like help with cooking or shopping, many people

'One of my friends said "I can go through paperwork and I've got the weekend free. Let me know what you need me to do." It was such a relief, because I knew he meant it and wasn't just being polite.'

will say no. However, if you say 'we're going to the supermarket, can I get you anything?' or 'I've just made a casserole – we have plenty to spare', the bereaved person may be more likely to accept your offer.

You could also offer to break the bad news to other friends or acquaintances on their behalf. When coping with shock or intense grief, it can be difficult for the relatives or friends of the person to relay the information, especially when there are many people who must be informed. That said, it is wise to consult the deceased's family before doing things on their behalf.

It is worth remembering that many people are flooded with offers of support and practical help in the months and weeks following a bereavement. Surprisingly, this is often when people are best able to cope – shock can prevent grief from taking hold and the offer of support can make the loss easier to bear. A few months later, the situation may be different. Unfortunately, people may assume that the bereaved person is coping or is now 'through the worst of it'. In actual fact, this can prove to be the hardest time, so it is worth bearing in mind that during this period the bereaved person may appreciate your support.

Saying the right thing

One of the first things people worry about is 'saying the right thing'. In fact, the bereaved person is often glad to know that you are thinking of them. Anna says:

'When my best friend lost her partner I felt totally useless. We'd previously been close, but she seemed to want to distance herself from me. When she cried I kept trying to think of things for her to do to take her mind off it. She told me that she didn't want solutions, she just wanted someone to listen.'

As Anna discovered, in the face of another's grief, we may want to 'fix' things and offer solutions. It may sound strange, but one of the hardest things to do can be to listen in a supportive yet not intrusive way. This means listening to what the bereaved person is saying rather than trying to make it better. If you jump to find solutions or try to cheer people up, it is easy give the message that you don't think it's okay for them to be sad. Counsellors and therapists can spend years in training learning to really listen to what they are being told.

This doesn't mean, however, that it is impossible without training – far from it. If someone is very distressed it can make us feel inadequate, and our natural instinct may be to try to console them. There is, of course, nothing wrong with this. However, it may be wise to ask yourself before you do something whether you are trying to save your feelings or theirs. Of course, not every bereaved person feels the same way, but here are some general things to avoid:

- Try to avoid 'looking for positives' in someone's death. For instance, if the death was an accident, a well-meaning friend might say 'well, at least they have now put in safeguards so it won't happen again'. There may be positive things to come from a loss, but the grieving person will find them in their own space and time.

- Don't ask the bereaved person to 'count their blessings'. They may indeed have a lovely family, their health and great friends but they are still grieving for someone that they will never see again.

- Unless you know the person well and are sure they really want to talk, don't press them to talk about their feelings. If they change the subject, try to follow their cue and talk about other things. They may be having a good day and don't want to be reminded of their loss at that particular moment.

- Don't forget to ask them what they need. Some people need to talk – some don't.

- It may sound callous but don't be too afraid to tell them about what's going on in your life. While it may be inconsiderate to off-load all your problems onto them, sometimes it can be comforting for people to hear about what's going on for those around them rather than talking about their grief.

'If you are struggling to cope, it is important to be honest both with yourself and the bereaved person about what you are able to provide.'

Listening and sharing

Caring or supporting someone who is bereaved can be emotionally, spiritually and physically draining. So far, we have talked about what to do when people won't take help. Sometimes, however, the situation can be reversed. The bereaved person may become very dependent on you to help them come to terms with their loss. Whether the support you provide is emotional or practical, this can be very tiring, particularly if you have problems to contend with in your day-to-day life. If you are struggling to cope, it is important to be honest both with yourself and the bereaved person about what you are able to provide. You needn't be confrontational, often a gentle reminder will suffice. Sometimes a bereaved person can be so consumed with their own grief that they are unable to see the needs of others. Vera says:

'After my husband died I was eaten up with grief. I was such a mess that even going to the supermarket seemed impossible. My lovely neighbour was a godsend – she brought round pots of stew for me, mowed my lawn and came round everyday to chat. This went on for months, and although I didn't realise at the time, I had become so dependent on her. It was almost like she filled the gap that Bert had left. One day she came round and seemed much quieter than usual. I asked her what was wrong and she explained that her grandson had been ill for a few months and had to have an operation. Only then did I realise that I hadn't asked about her family for months. I think that was the first time that I began to see past my own grief. Actually, being able to support her helped me to feel useful again.'

The neighbour hadn't said anything about her own troubles as she didn't wanted to burden Vera. She was, however, struggling to cope with her own problems as Vera came to realise. In actual fact, Vera started to feel a little better when she was able to return the favour and support her neighbour.

Summing Up

- When someone you care for has suffered a bereavement it is natural to feel helpless, worried, awkward or overwhelmed.

- There are a number of practical things you can do to show you are thinking of them, such as sending flowers, a card or writing a letter.

- Sometimes practical help is appreciated, whether it's company for a shopping trip or helping to sort out the deceased's belongings.

- Be honest if and when the help required by the bereaved person is too much for you to cope with.

- Don't feel you have to fix problems or cheer the person up – listening and being there can be just as important.

- If you are unsure what to do, ask the bereaved person what they need.

- Even if you feel awkward, don't be tempted to avoid the bereaved person. This can be very hurtful.

- Don't try to look for the good in the situation or tell them to 'count their blessings' – it may come across as insensitive. While something positive may come out of a loss, a bereaved person will find this in their own time and on their own terms.

Chapter Nine

Types of Loss

No matter what the circumstances or relationship, losing someone close is a devastating experience. There are, however, some types of loss which are particularly complicated, such as the death of a child or a bereavement in violent or traumatic circumstances. This isn't to say that these types of loss are somehow worse, rather that they pose a different set of challenges. This chapter is devoted to specific types of bereavement including the loss of a child, bereavement by suicide, violent or traumatic death and the loss of a partner.

Loss of a child

Losing a child is a parent's worst nightmare, and those that go through it have their lives changed forever. For most parents, protecting their child is the strongest instinct they possess, so when their child becomes ill or has an accident they feel that they are to blame. If a child dies they may feel that they should have died in their place. It can also feel like the natural order of things has been subverted when the young die before the old. Jillian:

'Oliver died a week after his sixth birthday, after contracting meningitis. It was the most devastating experience I have ever had to face. I felt like I didn't deserve to live when Ollie didn't have the chance to grow up. I had another child, Caitlin, with my new partner but because he wasn't Ollie's dad, I felt that he just couldn't understand what I was going through. Although I couldn't bear the thought of anything happening to Caitlin, I actually found myself jealous that Mike still had 'his' daughter. The strain on our relationship became almost unbearable, and it all came to a head when six months after Ollie's death, Mike moved some of the toys in his room.'

'For most parents, protecting their child is the strongest instinct they possess, so when their child becomes ill or has an accident they feel that they are to blame. If a child dies they may feel that they should have died in their place.'

As well as sadness, shock and anger encountered in any bereavement, parents may often have some of the following experiences:

- More protective of the lost child's siblings, being acutely aware of risk.

- Relationship difficulties with a partner.

- Guilty that they didn't protect the child.

In Jillian's case, she became worried that Caitlin would become ill like her brother had done and was frequently checking her for rashes. She also became very protective of her daughter and was afraid to leave her with a babysitter in case something happened when she wasn't there. Again, this is an understandable response, but can lead to the surviving child becoming nervous or fearful. Jillian's relationship with Mike also suffered as a result of Ollie's death – it is common for the anger over the child's death to be projected onto others which can put a great strain on personal relationships. However, where the child's biological mother or father was not in a relationship with the bereaved parent, they can find that they are drawn to each other in their shared loss. Unfortunately, difficulties can also arise when both parents of the child are in a relationship – even if they have been previously close. Sadly, this means that in some cases the relationship breaks down, as each person struggles not only with their own grief, but the grief of the other parent. However, many couples do find their way through their loss together and are able to mutually support each other. It is worth remembering that:

- People grieve in different ways. Your partner may seem to be coping but is actually struggling like you.

- Some people may find that they or their partner may be reluctant to talk about the death of the child, and may mistake this for indifference or lack of concern.

- When both people are grieving, it can be difficult for them to continue in the roles that they adopted prior to the bereavement – where one partner works, this can mean financial difficulties.

- When both people are grieving, household jobs and chores may become a battleground.

In a single-parent family, you may feel that you lack support and that no one else can comprehend the loss you have experienced. Where you are not a caregiver, you may feel excluded from the grieving family, making it difficult to resolve your grief. If you have been estranged from your child, or your child was perhaps living with relatives or in foster care, this can make it hard to accept the loss – particularly if you had wanted or expected the child to return.

Things that can help:

- Parental support networks and child bereavement charities offer both practical and emotional support for grieving parents (see help list).

- While most parents feel that nothing positive could possibly come of their child's death, later down the line fundraising or making a commitment to a charity in their child's name can provide some comfort. Jillian, for instance, became involved with meningitis charities and worked to raise awareness of the illness.

- Although this can never compensate for the loss of the child, taking on new hobbies and interests can help to fill the hours.

Coping with bereavement by suicide

Losing a loved one as a result of suicide can be a profoundly traumatic experience. While it is normal to feel guilt when someone dies, in cases of suicide this guilt can become overwhelming – those left behind feel that they should have done something or intervened. Although some of these emotions are common to most bereaved people, death by suicide can leave you feeling:

- Angry.

- Punished.

- Traumatised, particularly if you found the body.

- Guilty.

- Ashamed.

Many bereaved people feel anger. However, in cases of suicide this feeling can be particularly strong. After all, you might think the person has chosen to leave. For this reason, people living in the wake of suicide often describe the

'The person who has died was likely to be suffering from depression, stress or other pressures and, more often than not, the decision to take their life was not a direct result of what one person said or did.'

deceased person's decision to take their own life as the 'ultimate rejection' of those they leave behind. In reality, however, the situation is usually more complex. The person who has died was likely to be suffering from depression, stress or other pressures and, more often than not, the decision to take their life was not a direct result of what one person said or did. It is worth remembering that the mental situation of someone who decides to take their own life is likely to be in a state of turmoil and the thought of hurting those who care about them is probably far from their thoughts. Tim:

'After my son killed himself I had to deal with people's questions. They all wanted to know why he had done it. To be honest, I still don't really know. He was off at uni and seemed to be having a good time – every time people asked I just felt totally useless, like I'd failed as a parent.'

Tim's experience is not uncommon amongst survivors of bereavement by suicide. Even today, there continues to be a stigma surrounding suicide and many people can feel a sense of shame about what has happened. This can be exacerbated in cases where it is unclear why the person decided to end their life, and without answers it can seem impossible to move forwards. The road to healing after someone you love has killed themselves is long and hard, but it can help to know that you are not alone. There are support groups throughout the UK which allow individuals who have been bereaved by suicide to meet, share stories and support each other in their grief. There are also specialist bereavement counselling services (such as Cruse) which can help you to cope with your grief. You'll find more details on these in the help list.

Living with violent death

When someone dies as a result of crime or violence, the anger, disbelief and shock can feel overwhelming. The death may have been senseless, unjust or simply a case of being in the wrong place at the wrong time. Alternatively, you may know those who are responsible. Either way, you are likely to feel justifiably angry – particularly towards the people who caused your loved one to die. Selena's parents died in a road traffic accident when she was still a teenager:

'I couldn't believe it. Just because someone had had too much to drink one evening my family was gone. It made no sense – how could this happen to my parents? I wanted the drunk driver to suffer like I had and I think I would have killed her if I'd had the chance. I wanted to see her punished but after she was sentenced I didn't really feel relieved, just numb.'

For many people, seeing the perpetrators brought to justice can bring some degree of relief or a sense of closure. For Selena, the thought of the drunk driver being punished kept her going in the months following her parent's death. However, the sentencing of the perpetrator was just part of the process – she still had to find her own way through her grief. Losing someone this way can be very lonely. Friends and colleagues may have experienced bereavement but are less likely to have lost someone in the same way. For this reason, it can be very helpful to get in contact with other victims of crime. Some of the organisations listed in the help list will be able to help.

Trauma

Trauma is a word used to describe the negative effects that a dramatic event has on our wellbeing. The traumatic event is often re-lived in the mind through flashbacks and dreams. When someone commits suicide, it is often someone close to them who finds the body. This is something that is very hard to come to terms with, and the image may stays with you for weeks, months or even years. Similarly, if a loved one died a violent death, it can seem impossible to erase the details of the event from your mind even if you weren't actually present when they died. Post-traumatic stress disorder (PTSD) is the name given to the condition which can follow a traumatic event. The symptoms include:

- Flashbacks (when an everyday experience triggers a vivid memory of the traumatic event).

- Nightmares (which tend to recur frequently, sometimes every night).

- Panic attacks (that have started as a result of the event).

- Anxiety.

- Obsessive thoughts surrounding the traumatic event.

'I couldn't believe it. Just because someone had had too much to drink one evening my family was gone. It made no sense – how could this happen to my parents?'

You may find that you simply cannot get what has happened out of your head and may frequently feel shaky, nauseous and anxious. However, although the symptoms are severe, the good news is that there are people out there who can help. Your first port of call should be your GP who can refer you for counselling and/or prescribe medication to temporarily reduce your levels of anxiety. If you feel that you are reaching crisis point it is vital to get professional help as soon as possible, even if this means going to your nearest A&E department. You can also use phone support services – the Samaritans are a voluntary organisation who will answer your call at any time of the day or night. You'll find their contact details in the help list.

When your partner dies

Whether married, unmarried, co-habiting or living apart, losing a partner has a dramatic impact on the person left behind. Many couples come to depend on each other emotionally, financially and spend most of their leisure time together. It is therefore natural to feel lost if your partner dies, no matter what their age or the length of your relationship. If you have children together you may also have to adjust to life as a single parent. This might mean that you are now under pressure to become the sole breadwinner as well as managing childcare at a time when you are struggling to cope emotionally. Although it is probably the last thing that you want to think about, your home and finances will be some of the first things you have to consider, particularly if you have been solely supported by your partner. Chapter 2 provides more details on how to manage these practical concerns. Practical matters aside, adjusting to life as a single person is likely to be daunting and presents a number of challenges. Some people enter into new relationships relatively quickly, while for others this remains absolutely unthinkable. There is, of course, no hard and fast rule as to when and whether it is right to enter into a new relationship. The danger is, however, that the need to fill the huge gap left by your partner overrules the normal reservations you might have towards the new partner. Losing your partner is undoubtedly a devastating experience, but there are things you can do to take care of yourself during this difficult time:

- Give yourself time and space to grieve. Sift through old photographs or keep their clothes in the wardrobe – whatever helps you to cope.

- Try to allow friends and family to support you, even if you are used to only confiding in your partner.

- If you have children together, creating a memory book with photographs and mementos can help children to talk about loss and understand their feelings. The book can also be saved when they are older and may want to know more about their mother or father.

- Local groups for those that have lost a partner can prove a great source of support (see help list).

Summing Up

■ Every bereavement presents a different set of challenges for those left behind.

■ Whatever the circumstances of your bereavement, there are organisations out there that offer both practical and emotional support.

■ Death as a result of suicide or violence can lead to trauma. Post-traumatic stress disorder requires professional treatment.

Chapter Ten

Looking to the Future

Developing a support network

How people cope in the long term following a bereavement is, in part, determined by the support networks in place to help them. So what is meant by the term 'support network'? Simply put, it is any group of people who can help or support you in the weeks, months and years following the loss of a loved one. Here are some examples:

- Self-help and support groups for survivors.
- Counsellors and psychotherapists (more on this in the next section).
- Friends and family.
- Friends/family of the deceased person.
- Helplines and bereavement organisations such as Cruse.

The role of friends and family

Friends and family are likely to be the first people available to offer support. They can provide a sympathetic ear and practical help in the months following a bereavement. However, some people find relying on immediate friends and family as their sole support network places too much pressure on these relationships, particularly if these people also knew the deceased and are struggling to come to terms with their own grief. However, no matter how supportive, if they didn't know the deceased then it may be hard for them to understand your feelings as Susie discovered:

'A support network is any group or groups of people who can help and support you in the weeks, months and years following the loss of a loved one.'

'My family were great when my best friend died – they supported me as well as they could but I found it hard to talk about Keira because they didn't know what she was like – she was effectively a stranger to them. Once every few months I meet up with Keira's other friends – I didn't know them very well before she died, but I find that what we all have in common is knowing Keira. We have a good time and it helps me to feel close to her.'

As Susie found, sometimes unexpected people can help as part of your support network. In Susie's case, seeing Keira's friends allows her to remember aspects of her friend's life that she couldn't share with her family. However, in cases where other family members are also grieving, finding support outside the family can prove useful.

Self-help groups

If you have suffered a bereavement in particularly traumatic or difficult circumstances (such as suicide or crime, for instance), a support group can provide one of the few opportunities to connect with people who have had a similar experience. There are a number of organisations that can help, see the help list for a selection of them. Your local authority, council or CAB may be able to provide you with details of organisations nearby. Many of these are support groups which meet once a month or more often. At these meetings people come not only to share their grief and give and receive support, but also to make new friends. Andrew:

'The group was really useful because after I lost my brother to suicide I felt like no one understood. Other people tried to empathise, but they hadn't lost someone in the same way that I had. Alongside the grief I also felt guilty, like I should have done something. I really clicked with the people at the group because they "got it".'

Each group will have their own policies and ways of doing things, so it is worth considering what sort of approach you might find useful. Attendees of self-help or support groups report that it is a relief to be in the company of others who actually understand what it is that they are going through. Self-help groups can be roughly divided into two different types:

- Formal – these groups are often led by a trained psychologist and/or counsellor. Some are available through the NHS, although provisions vary from one part of the country to another. In these sessions, sometimes referred to as 'group therapy', the leader will offer exercises and members will be invited to share their experiences. Sometimes the emphasis is placed less upon making new friends and more on therapy work. Again, this will vary from group to group.

■ Informal – these are usually organised by individuals without a professional background in bereavement and are offered as a way to support and/or counsel each other. There will often be a group leader who will invite the members to participate. There may also be a meal, coffee or tea beforehand.

Either way, the aim of these groups is to offer bereaved people a safe place to mourn and work through their feelings. While many people find these groups a real source of comfort and support, there can be some limitations:

■ People with severe depression or undiagnosed mental illness may not receive the support required, especially if the group is of the informal type. Sometimes these conditions may have existed before the bereavement, or else the loss may have triggered them. In these cases it may be necessary to seek medical help, or a mental health professional, even if this is alongside attending the self-help group.

■ In both informal and formal groups, dominant personalities may come to 'take over' the session. In these cases it is vital that the leader or organiser of the group has the skill to ensure that everyone in the group is heard and able to participate.

■ For fragile people, the grief of others may prove too overwhelming, particularly if they are just getting to a point when their own distress is manageable.

If you have trouble accessing these groups or are unable to find one suitable, you might consider starting your own. You might begin by putting a small advert in the local paper to gauge interest, asking people to email and/or phone to register their interest. Of course, these sort of groups are not everyone's cup of tea but for those who use them they offer:

■ A chance to meet people and make friends who understand some of what you are going through.

■ A chance to support other people in their loss.

- A way to get ideas from others as to what has worked for them in overcoming their grief.

- If you have suffered a bereavement in particularly traumatic or difficult circumstances (e.g. suicide or crime), a support group can provide one of the few opportunities to connect with people who have experienced anything similar.

If face-to-face meetings are too daunting or you struggle with the regular commitment, there are a number of national and regional organisations who operate phone lines for support. A number of organisations also offer counselling by phone. Aside from these organisations, there are also crisis lines such as the Samaritans who can support you. Phone lines offer the following advantages:

- You can choose to be anonymous and anything you say is confidential.

- You can share as much or as little as you like.

- You can offload your problems onto someone who won't burden you with theirs!

- You can use the service as and when it is needed – a regular commitment isn't required.

- You can speak to someone out of hours when you are distressed but no one else is available.

'A counsellor or psychotherapist is someone who is trained and skilled in listening.'

Counselling and psychotherapy

For many people, it can be too difficult to share bereavement with a group of people they have never met before. For this reason, counselling and psychotherapy can provide the opportunity for one-to-one work. The obvious advantage of this is that the therapist can turn their full attention to the person being counselled (often called the client).

A counsellor or psychotherapist is someone who is trained and skilled in listening. While it may seem easy just to listen, it can in fact be hard for many people to do so. Perhaps they want to share their own grief (if they knew the deceased) or bring in their own experience. They may also be embarrassed and awkward, or may try to offer what they see as solutions. A good therapist will do none of these things, as the aim is to help you to understand your own feelings and thoughts without trying to manipulate or influence them.

There are many different styles of psychotherapy, each with their own method and theory about what works best. If you are offered counselling from your GP, they may be able to recommend the type that is best for you or they may alternatively recommend what is available to them. Many NHS trusts make provision for cognitive-behavioural training. If you haven't got a referral from your GP, or are not happy with the service offered, there are many private organisations offering counselling – some of these work on a charitable basis, offering low-cost or free counselling. Others are more expensive, costing anything up to £35-40 per hour. Most will offer a first session at a nominal or lower price – this session will give you a chance to ask questions and to see if you 'click' with the therapist in question. It goes almost without saying that finding someone that you trust and like will enhance the work you are able to do together.

There are also organisations such as Cruse who offer their own programme of counselling, which is specifically designed for those suffering bereavement and grief. To get started, the first step is to find out what is available where you live. Ask for leaflets and/or information about the services offered and costs involved. Most reputable counsellors and psychotherapists will be registered with the British Association for Counselling and Psychotherapy (BACP). This organisation ensures that the service offered by their members is safe, accountable and professional. There are also rules about what different counsellors, at different stages in their training, are able to charge.

'Counselling and psychotherapy can help the individual to clarify their experiences and understand their own emotions.'

What is therapy?

Counselling and psychotherapy can help the individual clarify their experiences and understand their own emotions. This can often help people to cope with their grief and move forwards with their life. Unlike a medical treatment, most therapy does not seek to 'cure' an individual of their problem(s). Instead, the therapist will ask questions, point out connections and assumptions in the client's narrative. In this process the client is helped to find their own answers and solutions. Most importantly, therapy can offer you, the client, an opportunity to tell your story and be heard in a non-judgemental way.

Summing Up

■ A support network is any group of people who can help or support you in the weeks, months and years following the loss of a loved one.

■ There are many different types of support available to help bereaved people to come to terms with their loss.

■ Self-help or support groups can provide a rare opportunity to speak to others who have had similar experiences.

■ Phone lines provide out of hours support and are often completely anonymous.

■ Counselling and psychotherapy can help you to understand and cope with difficult emotions.

Help List

Age Concern

Astral House, 1268 London Road, London, SW16 4ER
Tel: 0800 00 99 66 (helpline)
www.ageconcern.org.uk
Advice and support for the older bereaved person.

Bereavement Advice Centre

Ryon Hill, Ryon Hill Park, Warwick Road, Stratford upon Avon, CV37 0UX
Tel: 0800 634 9494 (helpline)
www.bereavementadvice.org
This is a non-profit organisation which provides free advice on the practical
aspects of what to do when someone dies.

British Association for Counselling and Psychotherapy

BACP House, 15 St John's Business Park, Lutterworth, Leicestershire,
LE17 4HB
Tel: 01455 883300
bacp@bacp.co.uk
www.bacp.co.uk
A professional registering body for counsellors. Has a find-a-therapist
section. You can also call their client information line for help finding a suitable
counsellor.

Citizens Advice Bureau (CAB)

www.citizensadvice.org.uk
With branches all over the country, the CAB offers free advice on finance and
legal matters. Visit the website to locate your local branch.

The Compassionate Friends (TCF)

53 North Street, Bristol, BS3 1EN
Tel: 0845 123 2304 (helpline)
www.tcf.org.uk
This is an organisation of bereaved parents offering support to others after the death of their child. As well as the telephone helpline, TCF offers email and letter contact and information on support groups in your area.

Cruse Bereavement Care

PO Box 800, Richmond, Surrey, TW9 1UR
Tel: 0844 477 9400 (helpline)
helpline@cruse.org.uk
www.crusebereavementcare.org.uk
Cruse is a national charity which offers independent advice and support to adults and children. There are branches all over the country, many of which offer one-to-one counselling, a telephone helpline and support groups.

Department for Work and Pensions (DWP)

www.dwp.gov.uk
Information about benefits and how to cancel them after the recipient's death.

Directgov

www.direct.gov.uk
This is a government website which details all legal aspects of applying for probate and registering a death. It also has links to other organisations offering advice or assistance.

JobcentrePlus

www.jobcentreplus.gov.uk
Information about benefits and how to claim/stop them.

National Association of Funeral Directors (NAFD)

www.nafd.org.uk
Advice on organising a funeral and finding a funeral director.

National Association for Mental Health (MIND)

15-19 Broadway, Stratford, London, E15 4BQ
Tel: 0845 766 0163
www.mind.org.uk
MIND offers confidential mental health information, advice and can direct you to services in your area.

National Association of Widows (NAW)

www.nawidows.org.uk
This is a paid subscription service (£16 per year) for those who have lost a partner, husband or wife. NAW offers regular meetings, information, support, a befriending service and opportunities to participate in group holidays (at extra cost).

The National Society of Allied and Independent Funeral Directors (SAIF)

SAIF Business Centre, 3 Bullfields, Sawbridgeworth, Herts, CM21 9DB
Tel: 0845 230 6777
www.saif.org.uk
SAIF is a trade association whose members are all independent funeral directors.

Probate Registry

www.hmcourts-service.gov.uk/infoabout/civil/probate/index.htm
Forms part of the Family Division of the High Court. It deals with 'non-contentious' probate business (where there is no dispute about the validity of a will or entitlement to take a grant) and issues grants of representation. Regional office contact details are on the website, click 'contact us'.

The Samaritans

PO Box 9090, Stirling, FK8 2SA
Tel: 08457 909090 (helpline)
www.samaritans.org.uk
A voluntary organisation with branches all over the country, the Samaritans offer a 24-hour helpline for those experiencing any kind of emotional crisis. Some local branches also offer a walk-in service.

Survivors of Bereavement by Suicide (SOBS)

Tel: 0844 561 6855 (helpline)
www.uk-sobs.org.uk
SOBS offer advice, help and support for those bereaved by suicide. They can also direct you to support groups in your local area.

Victim Support

Tel: 0845 3030 900 (helpline)
www.victimsupport.com
National charity for victims and witnesses of crime in England and Wales, offering confidential advice and support.

Book List

On Death and Dying
By Elisabeth Kubler-Ross, Routledge, Oxon, 2009.

Overcoming Loss: Activities and Stories to Help Transform Children's Grief and Loss
By Julia Sorenson, Jessica Kingsley Publishers, London and Philadelphia, 2008.

Silent Grief: Living in the Wake of Suicide
By Christopher Lukas and Henry M. Seiden, Jessica Kingsley Publishers, London and Philadephia, 2007.

The Story of Babar
By Jean De Brunhoff, Egmont, New York, 2008.

Glossary

Administrator
The title given to the person who will organise the estate if the deceased person did not leave a will.

BD8 form
A form the registrar will give you. It should be sent to the DWP to inform them to stop any benefits and calculate any taxes (or rebates) due to the deceased.

Certificate for cremation
Issued by the coroner when the cause of death is deemed as natural, to allow you to cremate the deceased.

Certificate of fact of death
Issued by the coroner to enable the relatives to organise the will and funeral, whilst waiting for the body to be released by the coroner's office.

Coroner
The coroner is a lawyer (or sometimes a doctor) who has been appointed by the government to determine cause of death. They will also organise a post-mortem and further investigations (if they are judged to be necessary).

Estate
The deceased person's belongings, including any property owned along with their savings and assets.

Executor
The person named in the will, by the deceased, to organise the estate.

Grant of letters of administration
Where there is no will and more than one possible administrator, you must apply to the Probate Registry for a grant of letters of administration in order to organise the estate and access bank accounts.

Grant of probate
The executor will need to obtain a grant of probate in order to begin to organise the estate and gain access to bank accounts and financial details of the person who has died.

Humanist
A non-religious person who makes sense of the world using reason, experience and shared human values.

Inquest
A legal investigation that aims to clarify the circumstances surrounding a death.

Intestate
When the deceased did not leave a will.

Medical certificate of cause of death
Issued by the attending GP specifying the cause of death. You will need this certificate to register the death.

Post-mortem
An examination of the deceased's body.

Probate Court
If an administrator cannot be agreed upon, the case will need to be brought before the Probate Court.

Probate Registry
Appoints people to administer the deceased person's estate, where there is a will and where there isn't one.

Registrar
The person appointed by the government to record births, deaths and marriages. The death certificate will be issued by the registrar.

Secular
Non-religious.

Social Fund
A government scheme where you can get help with paying for a funeral if you are on a low income.

Need - 2 - Know

Available Titles Include ...

Allergies A Parent's Guide
ISBN 978-1-86144-064-8 £8.99

Autism A Parent's Guide
ISBN 978-1-86144-069-3 £8.99

Drugs A Parent's Guide
ISBN 978-1-86144-043-3 £8.99

Dyslexia and Other Learning Difficulties
A Parent's Guide ISBN 978-1-86144-042-6 £8.99

Bullying A Parent's Guide
ISBN 978-1-86144-044-0 £8.99

Epilepsy The Essential Guide
ISBN 978-1-86144-063-1 £8.99

Teenage Pregnancy The Essential Guide
ISBN 978-1-86144-046-4 £8.99

Gap Years The Essential Guide
ISBN 978-1-86144-079-2 £8.99

How to Pass Exams A Parent's Guide
ISBN 978-1-86144-047-1 £8.99

Child Obesity A Parent's Guide
ISBN 978-1-86144-049-5 £8.99

Applying to University The Essential Guide
ISBN 978-1-86144-052-5 £8.99

ADHD The Essential Guide
ISBN 978-1-86144-060-0 £8.99

Student Cookbook - Healthy Eating The Essential Guide
ISBN 978-1-86144-061-7 £8.99

Stress The Essential Guide
ISBN 978-1-86144-054-9 £8.99

Adoption and Fostering A Parent's Guide
ISBN 978-1-86144-056-3 £8.99

Special Educational Needs A Parent's Guide
ISBN 978-1-86144-057-0 £8.99

The Pill An Essential Guide
ISBN 978-1-86144-058-7 £8.99

University A Survival Guide
ISBN 978-1-86144-072-3 £8.99

Diabetes The Essential Guide
ISBN 978-1-86144-059-4 £8.99

View the full range at **www.need2knowbooks.co.uk**. To order our titles, call **01733 898103**, email **sales@n2kbooks.com** or visit the website.

Need - 2 - Know, Remus House, Coltsfoot Drive, Peterborough, PE2 9JX